PROFESSOR AT BAY

Professor

at

Bay

By BURGES JOHNSON

Essay Index Reprint Series

originally published by

G. P. PUTNAM'S SONS

BOOKS FOR LIBRARIES PRESS
FREEPORT, NEW YORK

First Published 1937
Reprinted 1970

STANDARD BOOK NUMBER:
8369-1520-8

LIBRARY OF CONGRESS CATALOG CARD NUMBER:
73-107718

PRINTED IN THE UNITED STATES OF AMERICA

CONTENTS

Contents

PROFESSOR AT BAY

Chicken Feathers

MY MIND, most excellent Theophilus, is like an
untidy henhouse, full of chickens which jostle each
other upon the roosts. When I try to capture one she
flutters about, making a great pother, and generally
escapes me in the end. The floor is littered with drop-
pings, though gay feathers and bits of fluff are scattered here and there. Last night I thought I had firm
hold on a trim little bantam of an argument, but he got
out of my hands, leaving me with one or two colorful
tail-feathers that I petulantly flung away. There is no
meat in a feather; and one needs many of them to
weave into something worth noticing. But now I have
gathered up several of them again and think that I have
a book.

————

What might have been considered random thoughts
are arranging themselves in some sort of pattern, as

though a dog had been circling to find a trail. Will you be patient with me, most excellent Theophilus, while I circle?

Some acquire wisdom by meditation and an inward scrutiny; others by considering the ways of the ant or the motions of the planets. Some envision a god, personifying omnipotence and omniscience, and enter into communion with Him, testing their own logic or their dreams against His calm remoteness. As for me, whatever grains of wisdom I may ever gain must come from contacts with my kind. Acquaintanceships, friendships, loves; hatred, sympathy, tolerance; conversations, discussions, disputes; admirations and repulsions that must be justified or destroyed;—out of these human relationships such philosophy as I acquire must be born.

II

Axioms

CONTROVERSY is to me so needful a discipline and so
pleasant a pastime that I do not care greatly which
side I am on, so long as it is the opposite side. One
would suppose, then, that in these days of social, political and economic upset I could live very happily.
But the truth of it is that the other fellow's axioms are
destroying all my pleasure. I want to treat them as
hypotheses and he will not let me. Often he opens
debate with an untruth,—"You know as well as I
do—" Since I do not know it as well as he does, I
cannot argue; I can only contradict, and that is a bad
beginning.

Furthermore, my next step must be to question his
axiom; which means that our argument has turned
sour almost from the moment of its serving. For a
man's loyalty to his axioms is so great that emotion
replaces logic when they are attacked. If he is a scientist
he views me with pity, since evidently I am not familiar

with the elementary truths conceded by Science. If he is a moralist he views me with horror, since I am questioning Revelation. If the question is social or economic he views me with contempt, since I am plainly unaware of those simple truths which have long been acknowledged by the Best Minds.

These social debaters are the worst of all, if their axioms happen to be maxims or "old saws." I might question an elementary scientific assertion, and if my opponent be patient he will take time to prove the equation. The moralist may be imbued with missionary zeal, plus optimism; he has my soul to save. But if my opponent has opened debate by saying "You know, just as well as I do, that honesty is the best policy" or "a stitch in time saves nine" then we might as well stop. I may question science, or doubt the authenticity of a gospel, but I must not contradict folk-lore. It is too portentous. I want to ask, "Who said that first—a prophet or a poet?" but of course nobody knows, and I am proving myself out of step with the human race.

Yet I must insist that a man gains self-respect every time he doubts an old saw, even though he loses the respect of every one else. Some one has called them the "crystallized commonsense" of the race. But they are quite as likely to be its jelled ignorance. The great advantage of them in argument is that they may mean almost anything one wants them to mean; or else be too obscure to have any meaning, which makes them especially valuable. "It's a long lane that has no turning" may mean that even the longest lane must turn, sooner or later; or it may mean that the lane which never turns seems very long indeed. "A rolling stone gathers no moss" is important only if the moss is important, and is disproved by every successful prospector. "Pride goeth before a fall" is misleading. It is pride that precedes and induces getting up. Perhaps one fault with such axioms is that there has been too much effort at condensation. One word in nine may have saved time, but truth has been overlooked in the process.

An axiom is an established fact, so obviously true that it needs no proof. Two of our most respectable and respected dictionaries say that it is "a self-evident fact"; but since I do not know what that means, I count it a poor definition. An axiom is always true; John Stuart Mill calls it a "generalization from observation." An hypothesis, on the other hand, may be true sometimes; wherefore the scientist begins to inquire about it, to see whether or not he can turn it into an axiom.

"Things which are equal to the same thing are equal to each other" is an axiom; but that "all men are created equal" is an hypothesis. That "a straight line is the shortest distance between two points" is an axiom; but that "a soft answer turneth away wrath" is hypothetical.

The axioms of exact science save time and a lot of unnecessary reasoning. "In science," says Wiggam, "you can depend on what the other fellow tells you. You can add it to your own stock-in-trade; what is more, you can make it your starting point for new conquests of the unknown."

But the social sciences are not yet exact enough, or scientific enough, to have any axioms of their own. In morals or economics or politics or social problems every sincere reasoner has to begin at the beginning. This is a pity, because most of us consider ourselves keen thinkers in at least one of those fields; yet we are so lazy, mentally, that we want to be spared as much preliminary thinking as possible. We like to start somewhere near the end, and jump from there to a conclusion, pretending that we began with a "self-evident fact." We collect easily memorized axioms for this purpose, and this makes us eager victims of any propagandist who skillfully coins them and utters them in a tone of finality.

The moralist, too, is an adept at this business of floating spurious coin. He even makes religion his unconscious accomplice, by turning all the old texts into axioms. "It is not good for man to live alone" used as the axiomatic foundation for an argument has led many a good man astray. "Train up a child in the way he should go and when he is old he will not depart from it" has been the axiomatic foundation for whole systems of education. Just as the pure scientist may begin with an axiom because he believes that scientific authority supports it always, so the moralist begins with a text, his tone implying that to question it would be impious. As a seeker after truth, he is seldom humble, so often is he sure that Omniscience is whispering in his ear or dictating to his pen.

The exact scientist is much less inclined toward axioms, and more toward hypotheses; so that when an Einstein attacks the root of his physics, or a Chamberlain upsets his nebular theory he cheerfully begins to rebuild the whole structure of his reasoning from its very beginning. But when the axioms of the theologician are attacked, eight times out of ten he prefers not to listen. If a scholar suggests that "train up a child *according to his bent*" better translates the original, he is attacking a corner stone of the whole educational structure which was built by moralists. Let us cling to the old axioms, and let well enough alone. Besides, the English of King James is more euphonious.

Personally, I do not object to the moralist. His conclusions are so utterly unprovable, anyway, that I am quite content to let him speak with a voice of authority. His sonorous guessing is as good as mine. Whether or not I shall believe him will be determined by emotion rather than reason; or else by the constituency of my blood corpuscles. Such convictions as I possess in the realm of morals are mine because I cannot help myself; in fact I should be much happier without some of them which my reason assures me are absurd.

But the greatest and most disturbing counterfeiters of all are the social, political and economic propagandists. Professors and lay-reasoners are equally bad; each has his favorite way of sinning. The professors would have us believe that psychology and sociology and economics are in truth sciences, each with its axioms supporting a body of exact knowledge. "Bad money drives out good" they asseverate. "Every effect must have a cause"; "No child should ever be spanked"; while we nod our heads and meekly jump after them. Laymen, on the other hand, are playing with vocabularies that they have never mastered, and inventing axioms to suit their own convenience, which by constant repetition they persuade us lazy-minded listeners to accept.

So it comes about that in this day when every one should be joyously debating, I find myself in a state of sullen rebellion. Word-combinations which other men put together are forever forcing me into positions against which my mind protests—when it is awake. For I know that when I accept axioms my mind is slumbering.

At this present moment of writing my self-respect is making its last stand against the political slogan, that bogus equation which is dinned at me until sooner or later I shall accept it—if not as the gospel, at least as an old saw. For a slogan is a spurious axiom, with half of the equation inferred. Its business is to make me avoid thought. "It floats" and "they are toasted" imply axioms that soap which floats is purer than soaps which do not, and that it is good for tobacco to be toasted. When the "full dinner pail" was tied up to the name of a political party, thousands of men voted that ticket without stopping to question the implied axiom that a High-protective-tariff equals Food-for-all. Most of us prefer to consider such statements axiomatic rather than hypothetical; because we would rather accept them and go on from there, than to be forever bothered by having to reason behind them. Besides, they are said so often, and remembered so easily that they must be true.

It is hard for me to forgive a certain great leader for happily tossing the phrase "boloney dollar" into the midst of popular controversy. The equation was obvious and its meaning clear; doubtless thousands of lazy-minded folks seized upon it as an excuse for avoiding all effort to think behind it. They began there, and went where it pointed. "Rugged individualism" is another. The complete equation may be stated positively or negatively. "Individuality equals ruggedness. When one disappears, so does the other." But how does anybody know? The Pilgrim fathers were collectivists; members of the Oneida Community were communists; the settlers of Utah and adjacent states were fascists; and all were painfully rugged.

If there are to be any axioms at the start of our argument, I want to coin my own. I rather like the idea of "rugged collectivism," for instance. It suggests Athos and Porthos and Aramis,—all for one and one for all. It is opposed to effete and effeminate individualism,— men shyly scattered into their several corners with their thumbs in their mouths. The pioneers were always collectivists; they helped each other clear the forests and build houses.

I am prepared also to assert, as axiomatic, that "competition is the death of trade." For I have seen three job-printers in a little town that might support one in comfort, all evidently believing in the gospel of competition, and all virtually bankrupt; while other trade in the town suffered because they could not pay their bills. I have seen four churches in a village that could hardly support one, all pathetically competing for customers and all dead without knowing it. In every corner of the land I have seen colleges competing for students, to the spiritual as well as financial injury of them all.

I like also the axiom that "all men were created unequal." It suggests a lively stimulating world, with men fighting to overcome their inequalities. If we all are equal, what's the use of going anywhere? There is no one to try to catch up to. It also seems to me axiomatic that "practice makes us more and more imperfect," because it pushes our standard of perfection further and further away from us.

So I intend to start debate with any axiom I please, and the fresher the better. If it is challenged I can have the fun of fighting for it. I am even prepared to begin with the axiom that one and one are three; because you know just as well as I do that there is sure to be a baby.

III

Argument's Henchman

Years ago, most excellent Theophilus, you will remember that I wrote an essay entitled "The Lost Art of Profanity," in which I urged not the abolition of oaths and such-like naughty words, but their conservation. My innocent argument had many repercussions, some of them still echoing. An earnest editor in New Jersey urged that the writer of such an article was no fit guide and counselor for Youth. Cartoonists pictured angry draymen shouting, "Goodness Gracious!" Best of all, a London newspaper cabled to ask what complaint America had against the vigorous Anglo-Saxon bequeathed her by the mother land; and then sent out reporters to interview London cabbies and Billingsgate fishwives to discover their attitude on the question. As many of them as were able to understand the inquiry seemed to be quite content with what they had.

After all of that turmoil and the intervening years,

one hypothesis remains.in my mind so undisputed that it has become an axiom: *emphasis destroys itself.*

Yet logic seems so frail a weapon against emotion! Those who trust to it make headway as slowly as those who trust to education. One must reach the end of a debate somehow; and if I cannot drown out my opponent by shouting louder than he does, I must, like Sir Toby, cow him into silence by a terrible oath with a swaggering accent sharply twanged off that gives my argument more effect than very proof itself would have earned it. But alas! the worst oaths I know are but stuffed clubs; and in the case of most of them the stuffing is coming out.

IV

New Maledictions and Cuss-Words

WHEN man began to lose his belief in a petty-minded, interfering god, then oaths and curses began to lose their true value. Enemies hurling curses at one another had to believe that each curse had the backing of some sort of Omnipotence, or it could not amount to much. Perhaps it was not so important for the man who hurled the curse to believe in it; but certainly the man at whom it was hurled ought be convinced of its authority.

As the conviction slowly died out that there was a god ready at a moment's notice to take sides in any small quarrel, the sonorous old oaths dwindled. "By God's Mercy!" shrank to "Gramercy"; "By God's Death!" became "Odsdeath," "God's Wounds!" became "Zounds," and finally along with them a sturdy lot of profane relatives went down into complete oblivion. The Goodness and Graciousness of Deity still serve the ladies for mild emphasis; "Dio Mio" has become "dear me"; "A pox upon you!" has been vaccinated out of existence; and "May you be condemned to eternal torment!" has shriveled into "damn." In fact the only real oath we have left must be galvanized daily into life by perjury laws. Even the bootleg profanity of yankee Calvinists who thought they might hurl God's name without His knowing it—gee, gol, gosh and godfrey—is no more today than the trash of speech, undeserving a capital letter or an exclamation point.

Yet until recently there lingered about some of these tattered and soiled fragments of an abandoned theology a sort of mystery, an aroma of power. They ceased to be curses, but they continued as cuss-words. Their value lay in the fact that those at whom they were hurled, while having no idea of what they once meant, still sensed a malign significance. At their worst, when they were made up of words which were socially ostracized, they became maledictions, or Bad Words. A malediction, I take it, is an invocation of evil from no omnipotent source, but a sort of home-made defilement. Little boys who use any of them have their mouths washed out with soap.

One other dwindling heritage remained to us from a form of cursing which was the most ancient of all; when man called upon Deity to turn his enemy into a pig or an ass, or any other creature lacking social status.

This form of execration still survived as "epithets," or the calling of names.

Please note that I have been employing a past tense. For in this present day of unrestrained emphasis, even the surviving cuss-words, maledictions and execrations of ancient and half-forgotten lineage are dying of anemia, sharing the fate of zounds and gramercy and 'sblood. There seemed to be little left that a man might use against his adversary except logic, and that of course is out of the question.

But man must have words to hurl; and I am suddenly aware that a new vocabulary of vituperation has been born while I slept. Its terms perhaps lack the authority of the old oaths and curses. But at least they are cuss-words. They have all the requisites: neither the cusser nor the cussed knows just what they mean; and yet there clings to them a certain mystery, a malign portentousness.

Plutocrat! Bolshevik! Capitalist! Communist! Pacifist! Imperialist! Militarist! Fascist! Radical! Rotarian! Bourgeoisie! Petite-bourgeoisie! Proletariat! Hurl one of these in the proper tone of voice, and the cussed shrinks back as from a blow, while the cusser gains all of that spiritual relief which was once enjoyed by the militant churchman who cried, "Anathema, maranatha, maledicta!"

No dictionary is new enough to offer definitions of these words based on current usage, for usage changes overnight.

A Plutocrat used to be one who ruled by reason of his wealth; but rich men in hopeless minorities, rich men who do not want to buy political power, rich men harassed and overtaxed, rich men in jail—all are plutocrats.

Bolshevik comes from a Russian word meaning majority. In America we believe that the majority should rule but that a Bolshevik shouldn't. A Bolshevik in Russia believes in Russia first—Russia for the Russians; down with foreign goods, foreign music, foreign capital, foreign labor! In America it is the Rotarian, so I am told, who believes in America first, and down with foreign labor and foreign goods. Ergo, a Rotarian is a Bolshevik.

A Communist is one who believes that all wealth should be held in common; that those who were lowest should be as the highest, and that those who were highest have no right to live at all. All power, they say, should be in the hands of the common people; and yet all communes, since time began, have been ruled by dictators.

An Internationalist is one who seeks to force our government to do something about the Jews in Germany, but either doubts or regrets the waves of emotion which swept our country at news of "Butcher Weyler's" concentration camps of starving women and children in Cuba. An Internationalist would make sacrifices for his household, and his village, and for all mankind; but not for his nation, as represented by "the flag." I have yet to learn his exact attitude toward county, state, congressional district and other political units.

A Militarist believes in a bigger and better army in order to avoid fighting. A Pacifist believes in bigger and better fighting in order to avoid the army. A Pacifist is, in fact, one who believes he should not resist a foreign foe, but would like to die resisting an American policeman.

Somehow, out of all this scrambled usage, I hope sooner or later to obtain definitions, and then will come power! For if you have followed my reasoning you must know that the strength of a cuss-word lies in its mystery. When I have them defined I may still hurl them with effect, but if they are hurled at me I am as Achilles.

An Achilles am I in truth, for I shall always have a vulnerable heel. That word "Bourgeoisie!" I shrink from it in argument. Give it just the right twist of pronunciation, stretched out, with a showing of teeth when you come to the "wah," and a hissing "z" sound to the "s," and I lie down on my back, metaphorically, and put all four feet in the air. When it is followed up in attack by Petite-bourgeoisie I am dead, and Proletariat buries me.

It does me little good to reason about these words, to say that they are used by people who borrow terms as well as arguments from an old-world situation and foolishly try to apply them to the new. Am I of the bourgeoisie? I can't be, unless there is aristocracy above me, and two "classes" below. Is it wealth that separates our superior from our middle class? Tell that to the old citizens of Massachusetts or of Virginia or the Carolinas, and then call out the marines. Is it birth? I have some *Mayflower* ancestors but I greatly fear me they were proletariat when they came over; and some Virginian forebears were lower than that, if there is anything lower than a proletariat. Is it rank? That comes into existence at the whim of the supreme authority; which would confine our uppest class to senators and representatives, or else to judges and post-office employees. It would depend upon whether you held that supreme power rested with the people or with Mr. Farley.

I have a Communist friend—he applies the term to himself—who says our three American classes are the exploiters, the exploited and (in between) the petite-exploiters—jackals, as it were, who run around after the lions. He says I am one of the latter. Why? Partly my attitude of mind, but chiefly because my slender savings are invested in stocks and bonds, which represent the sweat of the toilers. He thinks it is my investments which determine my attitude of mind. My education or culture, he says, has nothing to do with it, and I wonder just what he implies by that. Patiently I pointed out to him that at various times in my life I have had traffic with plumbers, carpenters, mechanics and others who are said to exude perspiration; and in more than one instance I suspected that their investments exceeded mine, and that they exploited me.

He admitted that while there are undoubtedly three classes in America—otherwise how could a poor social agitator gain a living?—yet the members of our classes are regrettably lacking in class-consciousness and refuse to stay put. A banker in jail, I was told, working with a road gang, is still bourgeoisie because he wants to get out and get back to his exploiting. But a street-sweeper, who wishes he were not a street-sweeper but investing that banker's money, is still proletariat.

"There's glory for you!"

"I don't know just what you mean by 'glory,'" Alice said.

Humpty Dumpty smiled contemptuously. "Of course you don't—till I tell you. I meant 'there's a nice knock-down argument for you!' "

"But 'glory' doesn't mean 'a nice knock-down argument'," Alice objected.

"When I use a word," Humpty Dumpty said in rather a scornful tone, "it means just what I choose it to mean—neither more nor less."

So far as most of those new cuss-words are concerned I have gained some immunity. I have stopped shrinking. Not so in the face of another group. "Introvert!" "Complex!" "Moronic!" "Inhibited!" "Mind-Set!" "Habituation!" "Prepotent Response!" "Eye-cue!" As a very small boy it was my custom, if I found myself near some barnacled old salt who muttered hoarsely, "Avast there, blast your eyes!" to withdraw hastily and seek the purer companionship of my parents. I was taught that such words might be the heralding of a richer verbal onslaught, equally obscure but even more dangerous. Today, when I find myself in the company of some frail and inoffensive appearing schoolmarm, and she chances to murmur "Fixation!" or "Psychosis!" my early training reasserts itself and I seek safer companionship.

Once upon a time vituperation was cabined and confined. Strong words were for strong men. But times have changed. "Damn" is lisped from the cradle, and the vocabulary of youth has burgeoned. When the average young person of today really unlimbers, even an old sinner might better sound the retreat.

"Freudian Complex!" Here is a pair of expletives which, in combination, have almost the authority of an oath. Add "Libido!" and they become a curse. I have heard them from the lips of a young woman who watched me with the wide eyes of apparent innocence; and I knew they heralded a barrage that would cause that horny old salt of my childhood to blush through his tan, could he have understood it all.

There is an essay that I must write some day. It will be entitled "Is There Anything Left to Whisper About?" My thesis will be that some of the lost reticences had their value. But just how to prove it I have not yet reasoned out.

I think that I might one day learn to use some of these new maledictions and execrations, and attack my own contemporaries with them; but militant youth, thus armed, frightens me.

"My son," I protest, "I don't see how you could possibly consider doing such a thing!"

"In that case," he retorts, "your eye-cue must be subnormal." It is almost as though he had replied, "The-hell-you-say!" In fact, the enormity of what he might mean, if either of us understood, leaves me tongue-tied.

Cussing even in my day never meant much. But in those arguments where it was used, the one who used most, and pronounced it most emphatically, generally won. That is still true. In these latter days I have known an assemblage of parents of both sexes to engage in argument upon the upbringing of children, all contentedly talking at once; until some firm young person suddenly silences the lot of them by interjecting the word "Norm!" It is as unsafe to ask her what she meant as to inquire of a London cabby what he means by "Gorblyme." He would only swear again, and worse.

The old-time cussing had its source in theology. The lexicon of bright youth today is far richer, drawn as it is from sociology, pedagogy, and above all from psychology. Here is a science that seems to be all expletive. I myself have heard two vocal adepts in this field hurling at each other "Ideation," "Epiphenomenalism," "Panpsychism," "Psycho-physical Monism," "Inhibited," "Gestalt," until the air was shattered.

"Impenetrability! That's what I say!"

"Would you tell me, please," said Alice, "what that means?"

"Now you talk like a reasonable child," said Humpty Dumpty, looking very much pleased. "I meant by 'impenetrability' that we've had enough of that subject, and it would be just as well if you'd mention what you mean to do next, as I suppose you don't mean to stop here all the rest of your life."

"That's a great deal to make one word mean," Alice said, in a thoughtful tone.

V

Untangling String

ONE test of Truth is its eternal applicability. As an axiom, it is always true. But that does not mean it will be recognizable the moment we meet it. Nor can one force it upon any one else; one may only offer it.

Truths that I have recognized become my convictions. If I shout them at you, reënforcing them by resounding oaths, that may prove my earnestness, or else my annoyance because you are so stupid.

Each of us can remember apparently trivial incidents of childhood when we first came face to face with broken bits of eternal truth. I recall, for instance, that as a small boy I was once untying the string around a parcel, while my father waited patiently. It annoyed me to feel that he was standing there. My fingers grew clumsy and the task a little harder and longer. When finally I had the thing unwrapped, I saw that he had been waiting with an open pocket-knife in hand.

"I reached an important point in my education," he

said casually, "when I discovered that the time I would save by cutting a string was often more valuable than the string I saved by untangling a knot."

Here was a bit of philosophy that seemed directly to contradict "many a mickle makes a muckle" and "save the pennies and the pounds will take care of themselves"; so I pondered, and finally accepted it.

I suspect that truth forced upon an unready mind may often do more harm than good; because when wrongly interpreted it is far more dangerous than error. An x-ray photograph, the surgeons tell me, cannot err. But a wrong interpretation of it may lead a young surgeon into mistakes that, without the photograph, he never would have committed.

I have since spoiled a lot of good string and done nothing whatever with the time I saved thereby.

VI

A Bas La Liberté

COLUMBUS was a commonplace sort of fellow with only one idea. Other people in his day had exactly the same notion and never got anywhere with it. But folks jeered at Columbus, and disagreed with him, and got in his way, and so trained and developed the muscles of his will that he was able to carry his idea triumphantly down the field and across the goal line.

Martin Luther was a man of ordinary dimensions at first, with a full supply of human frailties. But men tried to stop him and suppress him, and as opposition grew more powerful he grew the bigger.

The pages of history are sprinkled with the names of men whose convictions fed upon opposition; and it is the contemplation of that fact that is making me dispirited. Can it be possible that the cause of truth suffers when there is too much tolerance? Might I too not amount to something if I could persuade more people to disagree with me? As a teacher I have plenty

of theories, and numberless views, and a few solid beliefs. But I am living in too gentlemanly a corner of the
world. People who disagree with my views just courte-
ously disagree and then let me alone. If only some one
would attempt to muzzle me I might become a force
for Truth.

Martyrs are as necessary now as ever they were; and
I am sure they are especially needed in the field of
education, where traditions are so greatly venerated.
Yet here, for instance, comes a powerful organization
of university professors which tries in the name of academic freedom to do away with martyrization. With
well-intentioned earnestness it builds up protections
which actually do so protect our more venturesome
spirits that they find themselves floating in compara-
tively placid harbors instead of battling storms of opposition. Columbus, with the backing of a Research
Foundation, and a cohort of sympathizers all socially
recognized, crying out to him, "Sail whenever and
wherever you like!" would have talked himself out in
some taproom along shore.

What my teaching spirit needs in order to make a
Columbus or a Luther of it is a few old-fashioned college trustees of the sort one reads about. In moments
of reviving animation my fancy can still create one. I
see him with domineering manner, little beady eyes,

and heavy jowl. He slips into my classroom one day with a hard smile of greeting and listens from a rear seat uncompromisingly. Suddenly he interrupts. "Am I to understand," he barks, "that you are opposed to the Palmer system of penmanship?" I rise to meet the situation, and with one hand thrust between the first and second buttons of my coat, the other resting gracefully on the desk, I answer him in clear tones,—"You are. I am."

"Then turn out the lights," he says. "The class is dismissed."

With only one experience like that to rouse me, I could fight for any sort of penmanship, vertical, spencerian or backhand; with two or three such trustees dogging my footsteps I could lead a crusade.

Being in such a state of mind, it is easy for me to believe that many of the minor social turmoils which get into the papers represent the effort of some mute inglorious crusader to find any old cause to crusade for; and that much of our authority-baiting results from the laudable eagerness of some undeveloped Will to find any convenient way of developing itself.

Circumstances have always been against me in this matter. Years ago when I was a youth in college some accident set my brain to functioning. Its processes were far from perfect, but still the wheels did go around, and something ticked. I turned my youthful scrutinizing gaze upon the subject of a personal religion, and at once proceeded to dismiss a large number of coventional beliefs. When the time for senior statistics came along I wrote myself down a "Scientific Monist" and then awaited the tragedy of a broken home. Nothing happened. "He has not received the pamphlet I sent him," I thought to myself. So I took another copy home with me on a short vacation, feeling that the break must come sooner or later and it might as well be now. My clergyman father was then preaching from an historic trinitarian pulpit in New England. I faced him in his little study, and while there was love and respect in my feeling toward him, yet I was convinced that truth must come first. "I am a Scientific Monist," I said firmly.

"So I had observed," he answered me in serious tones. "I had always hoped that we might have one in the family."

What was the use! Monism, scientific or otherwise, lost a crusader in that moment. But I hurried on, resolved that somehow I should probe beneath the surface of that kindly sympathy. "I find it impossible," I whispered, "to recite the Apostle's Creed."

"Then you really ought not to try," he replied.

"But," I urged, "I have dismissed so many of the

things you consider fundamental, that a serious break has surely occurred."

"I am glad to have you begin thinking," he smiled, "and it is just possible that you and I would still agree on some of the fundamentals."

What chance was there for a Peter the hermit after that?

A few years ago I gained new heart. That was when the Lusk Laws—or was it Rusk?—were enacted in New York State. Was I not a New York State teacher? I assembled in my own mind a number of things that I was sure would cause Mr. Rusk—or was it Lusk?—to distrust me. I formulated some sentences that exalted the right of free speech, and gibed at foolish legislators who would command the tides to cease their ebb and flow. What though some of my incendiary phrases had been used before by Samuel Adams, yet I girt up my loins with them. But I could not find enough intelligent people defending the Lusk Laws—or was it Rusk?—and I found too many who were amused by them. One can crusade against a great wrong or a great injustice and find one's own convictions deepening and intensifying as the fight progresses, unless the thing crusaded against happens to be funny. One may tilt even at a windmill in a spirit of exaltation, but not at a windmill which sticks out a silly pink tongue at you.

Many years ago at a famous eastern college for women there was a ban upon any organization of embryo "socialists." So a number of students were wont to meet in a graveyard adjacent to the campus and there carry on their discussions. The result was that graduates of that graveyard became militant crusaders in the cause of equal suffrage and made the world respect them for the depth of their convictions. How are we going to get that same zeal for the-truth-as-they-see-it into these youngsters of today? The club that had thriven in the graveyard died of inanition a few years later when the ban was removed and a comfortable meeting place was officially provided.

A few windmills scattered about our campuses might prove to be more educational than laboratories, so far as each young Don Quixote is concerned. Here and there in the old endowed colleges they still maintain a tradition of compulsory chapel. For want of something better, earnest young zealots have tilted at that for a generation, calling it compulsory religion. Can't we give them real metal to teethe on? Poor young things, born too late, they do not know what compulsory religion is! What they need is a militantly Calvinistic college president planting himself in the doorway of the campus church, flanked on either hand by strong-arm members of the Christian Association. Students filing meekly past him toward the dim aisles are questioned sharply. "Do you believe in Jonah?"

"No, sir," stammers a nervous youth, but with a chin on him that suggests the stuff martyrs are made of.

"Out with him," says the President, "silent meditation in his room for two weeks."

"Can you sing all the stanzas of Hymn 246 without mental reservation?" he says to the next.

"I am a Christian Scientist," is the proud answer.

"Torture him," snarls the President, "and see if he feels it."

"How about infant damnation?" he questions a third.

"I don't believe in any of those things. I want to be a Parsee or Fire-worshiper, and spend these meditative moments lighting matches in a dark corner."

"Hurl him into the deepest basement; feed him on bread and water!"

Under some such régime as that there might be on any college campus a revival of religious discussion such as has not been known since early Victorian days, and young fighters after getting themselves fired from college would go forth into the world fired for evangelistic work in modernist pulpits.

I have come to envy those people who can build up an opponent of straw and then attack him. If their imaginations are keen enough, the straw man in time becomes very real, and they learn to fight as earnestly as the best. If they somehow kill themselves in the struggle, I am sure that a kindly Deity with a sense of humor will take them finally into paradise as true martyrs.

I have found momentary cause for hope in this recent communist business. Unfortunately the creed of American communism does not appeal to the latent common sense of enough of our students for any appreciable number of young wills to teethe on it, before passing on to other meat. But there are thriving groups here and there; wherever there are enough Lusks—or are they Husks?—in the local legislature or among "downtown" business men to give the youngsters a run for their money.

But as for myself, I am turned loose in too pleasant a pasture. Even the most intolerant of my neighbors are much too gentlemanly. Of course, I might find plenty of physical battles going on, either on the side of the law or against it. I might enlist as a G-man and fight gangsters, or sail down the Hudson under a black flag and rob coal barges. But alas, I am getting a bit old for that; and such struggles do not build the mind and spirit into a great social force. I could chalk up on the door of a church, "To hell with the Pope!" or shout that I am a Seventh-day Adventist in the midst of a Presbyterian Sunday service; or prove my nudist theories in the streets of Schenectady. But if I were jailed for any of these things my troublesome common sense would tell me that it was as a nuisance rather than as a martyr. Nor can I build up the strength of my convictions as one of a mob. Beliefs curdle into prejudices behind a mask.

I cherish plenty of theories, and a number of views, and a few solid beliefs. But the world needs men with militant convictions, and I fear I shall never have many of those until some one tries to muzzle me. There is too little muzzling being done these days, at least right around here. Of course, there are the Husks in the legislature who now and then muster enough votes to get something passed that sounds like a gag law. But having only sham convictions themselves, they are neither intelligent enough nor bold enough to construct a real muzzle.

I have heard that there are colleges here and there in the land where students are told that they may not indulge in tobacco, card-playing, dancing, or unusual ideas; and their professors find that certain pathways of pure reason are blocked by signs reading "detour" or "thus far and no further." If I could get into that sort of place I might come to be heard from, if I did not starve first. But in the meantime I must really get out all of my convictions, dust them off, and look them over. Perhaps I haven't enough, and some of my trouble lies there.

VII

Democracy

FAITH is a proud creature. She asks no support from Reason, but attaches herself to a cause with calm indifference to the fact that Reason may oppose it. Immortality is a case in point. Reason has struggled against that conviction throughout the centuries, using as her allies the keenest scientists and the most profound philosophers until, over little periods of time among little sections of humanity, she seems to triumph. Then with quiet assurance Faith again wins, and more millions of men and women march toward death, convinced that they will live again.

So, too, with Democracy. Any one who depends solely upon the evidence is likely to find against it. Reason, pointing to a steady succession of new incidents and examples, can make a good case for almost any other system, from communism to absolute monarchy, and can apparently destroy the theory of Democracy by logic and ridicule and the evidence of the senses. But

Faith says otherwise; and Faith declares it first among my convictions.

Democracy suffers most at the hands of those advocates who approach the bar of public opinion with noisy argument, with oaths and maledictions. Faith speaks generally in quieter tones; but when her voice does ring out, the world listens despite itself.

It seems to be true that those of our leaders who have held to this faith, closing their minds, if need be, to the evidence of their senses, have in their time done most to further democracy's cause. It is as though the generality of people, wise and foolish, sensing a dominant faith sustained by a sublimation of reason, allows such a leader to have his way a little longer or a little more effectively, before he in his turn is destroyed.

VIII

Oaths for Others

A NEIGHBOR of mine, who seems to like me well enough
as a man, regards me with suspicion because I am a college professor. He has heard from many directions that
professors are feeding poisonous doctrine to young
minds. He knows that a college professor who breaks
loose from a campus and gets into the machinery of
government is as bad as a monkey wrench, or worse,
and he suspects that all professors are getting in a lot
of dirty work, destroying democracy.

"All of this unrest comes from somewhere," says my
neighbor, "and they've got it pretty well pinned down
to the colleges. Talk about the dangers of pink tooth-
brush! Every college activity is tinged with pink. Something has got to be done about it. Look at the way
these teachers kick about being put under oath to uphold the Constitution. I'd have them sworn once a
month!"

Just who or what creates a young "parlor pink" or a

"campus red" he can never know, with all his omniscience. One is made by one process, another by another. I had dinner not long ago with a group of student "liberals," and I noticed that one of them seemed
especially explosive.

"You're a radical?" I asked him respectfully.

"Oh, yes; I'm way over on the left."

"How did you happen to get that way?" I asked.
"What started you?"

"Well, it's like this; I'm going to graduate from this
place pretty soon, and then I hope I'll get a job. If I
do, I'm going to get married, and then I suppose we'll
have kids. After that happens, I'll have to be conservative as hell, so I'm going to be radical now."

My heart went out to him. His seemed a simple creed.
I must have felt that way myself once, and I wish I had
not grown so far away from it. In my undergraduate
days a good deal of student experimentation went on,
but most of it unfortunately was physical; groping inquiries were conducted into the ways of women and
strong drink. It is natural for an adventurous youth to
undertake such research, and often it is merely a matter of chance and good fortune if he does not carry it
so far that it leaves permanent scars. Nowadays there
is more intellectual inquiry than there was, and some
indulgence in the strong drink of new ideas. I would

rather have my boy dissipate his energies in that way than in the other. I would rather have him try to find out what it feels like to be an extremist in religion or cheap social dogmatics than to discover what it feels like to be drunk on cheap whisky. He can recover from both orgies, but the physical one is likely to leave more scars and less wisdom.

A college president has told of his own reactions when he stepped from industrial life into his present position. During his years in business, he had seen the soap-box orator selling his social nostrums at the noon hour, with youngsters from the factory crowded around him exchanging banter born of their own humor and common-sense. Gradually, he said, they built up some resistance to claptrap arguments. Then, said he, "I went to a college campus, where I saw great numbers of highly selected young men carefully protected from discussion of 'dangerous' topics, and sent out after graduation as a sort of hot-house product, quite incapable of sizing up the demagogue. It happened once that a radical speaker came to us, brought by some liberal group. Shortly afterward I received a violent letter from the father of one of our students; 'I would rather,' he wrote, 'have my boy hear Lenin or Trotsky than that man.' I wrote back that if I only could arrange for his boy to hear Lenin or Trotsky it might do more for his education than any other happening in his college course."

If I were a teacher of the social sciences, I should want the boys in my class-room to learn the differences between communist and socialist and fascist, and I should want the definitions formulated by some one in sympathy with each political system. I do not want to have the republican platform explained to me by a democrat. I have said all this to my neighbor and he has listened to that part of my statement which confirms what he already suspects, and his mind resists any other part which modifies it. So he wants to put me under oath.

I am not quite sure of my neighbor's background, but he says he is a good American. I say that I am another, and it is hard to make comparisons. I am a descendant of two or three of the little company who came over on the *Mayflower,* and of a large number of other immigrants of that period. The little group which settled in Plymouth seems to have set up a sort of communal state with land in common, enforced labor, and a distribution of profits. The group just to the north of them insisted upon a state religion and persecuted or banished those who differed. The experiment just to the south ran a good deal more to rugged individualism, under a charter which has not been replaced by a state constitution to this day, and has proved to be a most effective device for encouraging boss control in politics. My own ancestors seem to have been involved in each of those experiments and in a great many others. Every little while one of them broke away from the jurisdiction of the established government and joined a group which planned to try something a little different somewhere else, whether it was on lands purchased from the Indians at Oyster Bay or seized from them in Connecticut or cajoled from them in Pennsylvania. Some later ones may have gone further afield to help set up communistic experiments in Oneida or on the banks of the Mississippi. One of my ancestors helped to finance the colonial adventure against Louisburg, when men of Massachusetts, Rhode Island and Connecticut seized an impregnable fortress after many of them had anarchistically refused to march under appointed officers and insisted upon choosing their own, or having none at all.

If I had inherited only one quarter of the radical impulses of my forebears, my neighbor would view me with more than suspicion. If I dared quote some of the utterances of Thomas Jefferson against the Supreme Court, or of Samuel Adams against constituted authority, he would want to put me in jail.

But perhaps one may still be considered a good

American even though the heritage of militant protest-ant-ism has come down to him in a weak dilution. As with many of my fellow Americans, that ancestral impulse stirring within me now finds voice only in sundry growlings and whinings, or in a sort of plaintive expression of surprise when I see our governmental experiment working out in ways that are displeasing. In truth, I am far more of a conservative than I should like to be.

If heritage does not necessarily make one a good American, perhaps I can frame a partial definition that will win my neighbor's reluctant approval: reluctant, because he knows I am a college professor, and he will be searching for a joker in the bill of particulars.

Good Americanism is based on the belief that our form of government continues to be an experiment that is well worth while; that it resulted from an admixture of pure idealism, expediency, and common-sense; that those characteristics which are the outgrowth of ideal-ism must be held fast, as the means to our salvation, and those which resulted from expediency must be changed from time to time as expediencies change; that up to the present time most weaknesses which have developed, or actual failures which have occurred, have been due not to the structure but to the indifference or self-ishness of ourselves as citizens. And the irreducible minimum of our creed, born of pure idealism, is an equal chance for all, under the law, coupled with complete freedom of *opinion*.

"If that is your declaration of belief," says my neighbor, "why do you object to an oath of allegiance?"

My answer is that I don't. Let us have teachers' oaths, by all means, provided we swear *all of those who teach*.

It is quite natural for our present-day witch hunters to demand a teachers' oath. They know that a deal of thinking goes on in the schools and colleges, cynical rumor to the contrary; and not enough anywhere else. Thinking is always dangerous; it leads to questions, and the teachers are expected to answer. In their answers, say the censors, they must be prevented from sowing seeds of disloyalty in the minds of the oncoming generation.

We do indeed want these young people to believe this experiment is still worth while; that its fundamental principles are born of idealism wedded to commonsense; that the office of its chief magistrate is invested with a rare dignity; that the legislator has a high purpose which entitles him to honor among citizens; that the laws of a democracy demand obedience and respect. But if as a teacher I chance to mention the obligations of citizenship, or speak of the dignity of the presidency and the legislature, I may be answered by a gibing or cynical retort, backed by the authority of "Dad." I have a few hours a week in direct contact with these youngsters for a few weeks of the year. Dad has a chance at them all the rest of the time.

Human nature has its curious obstinacies. I remember, for instance, that a short time ago my neighbor disliked a constitutional amendment which had been passed by due process and was a part of our organic law. He felt that it infringed upon his personal liberties, and he asserted his individual right to disobey the constitution when it behaved like that, and he taught his sons to disobey it. He would have been the objector then, if I had proposed that he subscribe to an oath binding him to obey.

Why bring that up now, when I am not seeking ways of disobeying any of the forty-three sections? I merely want to remind him of these odd streaks of obstinacy which seem to weave through us all; then I will cheerfully swear my oath as a teacher, if he as a teaching-parent will subscribe to this:

"I solemnly swear that I will not, within the hearing of my children, so disparage the high office of the President of the United States as to lessen the honor in which they hold it; that I will not speak of any incumbent of that office in terms that outrage his dignity; that I will not bring charges against his character unless I myself have incontrovertible evidence of their truth; that when I start to make such accusations I will recall the fact that men quite as intelligent as I charged Washington with venality, licentiousness and disloyalty; Lincoln with offensive personal habits and corrupt politics; Cleveland with specific sins too many to mention; Theodore Roosevelt with epilepsy and drunkenness; Wilson with looseness of character; and I myself will not join that ignoble company of calumniators, despite intense partisan feeling. I solemnly swear that I will not set an example to my children of law violation by disregard of traffic regulations, or evasion of any sort of taxes, or the dodging of jury duty; and I will conceal it from my children if I fail in that first duty of a citizen —the casting of my vote; so help me, God."

I will gladly be sworn again if you will do something about the preachers. True, they do not wield the influence that once they did. The young people do not attend services in great numbers, and—generally speaking—an hour's service is almost the only thing that the church has learned to do well. It is attempting now, forced by dire necessity, to learn how to do other things, but these expedients are being devised a bit late in the day. This Sunday hour may be the one time in the week when religious feeling has right-of-way; and the preacher is granted full opportunity to stir it. Yet I have heard three clergymen on recent Sundays address audiences that contained a high percentage of young people, and all three discussed politics and economics, and pronounced judgments of no particular merit and no originality. I have heard other sermons on peace, where the argument was not a constructive one, urging substitutes for war; but rather an un-Christian effort to arouse fears of physical pain and death; coupled with disparagement of the sacrifice freely made by soldier-volunteers of former times. I suggest that the legislators put every parson on oath that he will use his opportunity in the pulpit toward the end for which he was trained. The preachers, it is true, may complain that the legislators are making unwarranted implications by requiring such an oath, but let them meekly acquiesce. The voicing of objection might justify a charge of heresy, or lèse majesté,—or something.

I will cheerfully subscribe to a teachers' oath formulated by the lawyers in the legislature, if I may write a lawyers' oath. It is true that some sort of oath is already administered to them, but it does not seem to take very well. It won't hurt them to have another. All the teachers in the nation could never do as much, by classroom polemics, to break down confidence in this democratic experiment as the lawyers can do in any community by destroying belief in an equal justice for all. My students know that it is easier for a rich man to get off than a poor man. I do not teach them this. They hear it said at home; they read it in the papers every day. The "law's delays" have always been a by-word. Now they have become a stench.

I sat at a lunch table not long ago in a circle of fellow citizens; two of them were eminent counselors, and one was a judge. Somebody said to one of the attorneys: "How did your case come out?"

"Had it postponed."

"Had anything new turned up?"

"No; I wanted to go fishing. Opposing counsel agreed because he knew that he might want to go fishing some time; and the judge agreed because he liked to fish."

Everybody laughed. Everybody there knew that delay might especially inconvenience the litigant; they also knew that postponements can be obtained for any trivial reason, and that if a client has wealth enough to get a "good" lawyer, even fishing can secure postponement after postponement until the poor fellow on the other side cannot afford to keep on.

It would do me no good to tell my students that such things are not so. Bar associations in every state of the union are admitting it, and appointing committees to suggest ways (least harmful to lawyers) of cutting down the law's delays and making justice more easily obtainable by the poor man, or even more inevitable for the rich! Governors are denouncing lawyer legislators who will not make straighter and plainer the paths to justice, and will make it more difficult for the wealthy criminal to escape. My students have somehow come to believe that the bar does not want to lose the rich pickings that come from well-to-do malefactors; and if I tell them that this is not so, they will not believe me.

I mentioned the newspapers. Jittery legislators have quite logically turned their thoughts toward the press from time to time; and they should do so, for the daily newspaper does far more to mold student opinion than all the textbooks put together. But it is one thing to curb a teacher's speech, and quite another to restrain the editor's printed word. The legislator does well not to monkey with editors; he needs them more than he needs the teachers next November. But perhaps a very little oath for the editors would not be amiss; it could be attached as a rider to some bill to lower the postage rates on second-class matter: "I solemnly swear that I shall hold it always as my first duty to convey the truth to the minds of my readers; that I shall not permit its distortion for purposes of entertainment or to increase circulation; so help me, God."

Producers of movies should also be included in my

program, of course. But I had not thought to include them, because the legislators have in their case gone much further and imposed censorship. Perhaps they feel that men who can launch upon the screen some of the drama and most of the comedies that appear today would not understand the nature of an oath. As for radio, that other great textbook, it is in the hands of a commission, and it is necessary only to swear the commissioners.

But did I mention legislators? Now I am getting down to business. They are the ones who have drawn my oath for me, and are requiring me to subscribe to it. They want to feel assured that I will not prejudice these future citizens against our democratic institutions. I want them to swear most solemnly that they will stop prejudicing the young against our senators and representatives and assemblymen. They have done and are still doing more to break down confidence in representative government than inadequate teachers, parents, preachers, editors and producers all added together. True, they already subscribe to an oath, but I shall write them another; and then I shall cheerfully subscribe to mine if they will as cheerfully subscribe to theirs.

"I solemnly swear that I will vote on each measure according to my best judgment of its merits, and not with a thought for the vote on next election day. I swear that I will not trade votes with any of my fellow members; that I will not delay proceedings by long speeches intended merely for outside effect; that I will not play politics, seeking to hamper or hamstring the opposition when I know that by so doing I am clogging the machinery and preventing passage of necessary measures; that I will not introduce foolish bills or encourage others to do so; that I will not so much as sit down to dinner with a lobbyist if he has paid for the meal; so help me, God."

Teachers who are protesting the teachers' oath overlook the implied flattery of it. We are teachers; everybody knows that we have queer notions. Is not this very chapter a proof of it? What is more, it is natural that we should have them. If a man keeps his attention fixed upon the binomial theorem, or the break-down of the atom, or the authorship of Shakespeare, he may give voice to some odd political theories when he comes up for air. You cannot make yourself an expert in one narrow field without the risk of producing half-baked notions on some other subjects. This does not apply alone to teachers: a man might concentrate so intensely upon automobile production that he would voice odd opinions when questioned about American history; or devote himself so closely to the manufacture of steel that he would be even less effective than the ordinary man as an art connoisseur. Teachers get to be that way, and no one knows this better than their own students. "Sure," says a boy, "he has funny theories about family life; I've been to his house, and I know. But there never was a better teacher of chemistry."

I am a teacher. This does not mean, as we too well know, that I succeed in teaching any one anything. It means only that I receive a salary from an incorporated institution which arranges for groups of young people to meet me in a classroom. What results from such meetings is, in any final analysis, quite beyond my control. You can lead young men to the lecture, but you cannot make them think—your way! But now at last, and at least, we teachers have this assurance,—that our legislators, God save them, are convinced that we exercise some unique influence over these, our charges. We should take comfort from that and be grateful. Such flattery deserves kindness in return, and the best I can offer is to suggest that no solon, chancing to pass by, listen at the keyhole when I ask the average American boy what he thinks of the average legislator. The answer that he gives I can most solemnly swear would be none of my teaching.

I am quite content to take the teacher's oath. I suspect that I have more than once administered a better one to myself even before the legislators got busy. It is really their next act that I dread. Perhaps they will make me swear to observe Mothers' Day lest I threaten the American Home.

IX

Absent-Minded Professors

You and others may be suspicious of college professors, most excellent Theophilus, because so many of us are undoubtedly queer. Your man-in-the-street especially is distrustful; he distrusts foreigners, for instance, because they are "different," and he hears about a great many odd professors. He forgets that a man who fixes his attention constantly upon one piece of research may get strange notions on matters outside his special field; and that this is as true of banking experts and farm experts and bridge experts as of teaching experts. So he saves up all the funny things he hears about professors and mulls over them, and retells them. Finally, when he reads that some professor has murdered his grandmother, the man-in-the-street says, "Well, now, isn't that just what you'd expect!"

Consider the enormous number of stories about absent-minded people. Most men who concentrate their attention upon a specialty become absent-minded about other things; yet one seldom hears the phrase "an absent-minded man"; it is always "an absent-minded professor." I have a large collection of such stories. I like the one about the teacher who strolled down the street from the campus, saw a colleague, and said, "Hello, John; have you been to lunch yet?" And John, bringing his mind back with an effort from Elysian fields or laboratory smells, answered, "Lunch yet? Lunch yet? which way was I walking when you accosted me?"

I have collected such anecdotes because I have an important notion about professors, and these stories all tend to prove my point. A teacher is hired to devote his attention to one special subject; he is too often over-conscientious and takes no time off. The professor who did not know whether or not he had lunched yet because he was thinking about Greek, had his mind just where it ought to be; his body was in the wrong place. A college professor is too often absent-bodied.

But consider the business man who sits at his desk while his secretary does his work for him; he may be thinking about last night's party or tomorrow's golf game. His body is where it ought to be, but Heaven alone knows where his mind is. No wonder he needs to have a group of professors in Washington watching over his welfare.

X

Statistit and Such-Like

IT IS a weakness of democracy to distrust its experts. This is due in part to jealousy rather than ignorance. Our democratic tradition has it that success comes as a result of dogged labor, or "sweat." We also allow for luck, or "striking it rich." Rail-splitting to our mind is the ideal background; if this is accompanied by the study of a few books by candle-light, so much the better. That much learning is within any one's reach!

But the expert has acquired a superiority which cannot be secured through mere plodding, or luck, or money, or votes; so we regard him with suspicion, and feel that there must be something undemocratic about him.

I myself confess to a prejudice against statisticians. There is nothing personal about it; and it proves me no whit wiser than the average of my fellow citizens. For a statistician is merely one kind of an expert.

The fact is that what we common folk really distrust is a theorist. No man, we say, can gain knowledge of a subject just by reasoning about it; practice is the only teacher. Josh Billings is our prophet when he cries out, "It is better not to know so much, than to know so many things that ain't so." Bankers and insurance men, railroad presidents, soldiers, journalists, and farmers boast that their fathers attained success by a process of trial and error; so the sons who are spared the trials assert their right to continue the errors,—theorists to the contrary, notwithstanding.

But having conceded this much, let me assert that we distrust our experts mostly because of their own faults. First, they won't speak our language; second, they are likely to talk too much at the wrong time; and third, they devote their minds so undividedly to one pursuit that they lose their common sense.

When an expert so exalts his favorite idea that he cannot see around it or over it—whether it be a tonsil, or a grain of wheat, or a submarine, or a collection of digits—then he gains his only social pleasure from conversation with other specialists of his own kind about their common subject. The next step is inevitable: a new language is born. For it is natural that a sort of verbal shorthand should develop which makes for scientific accuracy, and saves time.

But accuracy and time-saving soon come to be secondary reasons for using this patter. It serves as a mystic symbol, a fraternal "high-sign," an abracadabra admitting initiates into a secret brotherhood, and effectively excluding barbarians. It is an awesome experience for any common man to overhear the conversation between two profound specialists in penology, let us say, or adenoids, or foreign exchange. I omit mention of the higher orders of statistician, because they have probably gotten beyond the need for words of any sort, and talk to one another only on their fingers. The common man shrinks from the sound of this esoteric vocabulary as though it were a malign incantation, or resents it as though it were a taunt. He begins to feel like rejecting the expert's opinion even when he can understand it.

It is my observation that the narrower a specialist has become, the more he has recourse to this special jargon; so that he builds up one more barrier between his mind and the common human mind, exchanges less and less the currency of common ideas, and reduces still further his own quota of *common* sense. While he can still translate into his own tongue the material for his problems, he loses all ability to translate his results back again into the vernacular.

Of course Heaven sends us in every decade a few specialists who keep themselves generally informed, and have a command of common, everyday English; they are often martyred, and oddly enough it is their own fellow specialists who hurl the first stones. But the narrower ones—those who fill their minds so full of uncommon sense that there is no room left for the common variety—are the ones who help to destroy popular confidence in experts by talking out of turn. Perhaps one wins world-wide recognition as a builder of locomotives, or as a leader of armies. This recognized special knowledge gives to any of his pronouncements a wide hearing. Whereupon he is induced to voice silly views of art or history or politics; and a scornful public cries "I told you so," and begins at once to distrust even the man's profound special knowledge, and the profundity of all other experts as well.

But getting back to statisticians: there is no such thing anywhere on this footstool as a two; nowhere can there be found, in the heavens above, or in the earth beneath, or in the waters under the earth, a three or a four. These are not things—they are figments of a mathematician's dream. When the user of them constantly remembers that they represent or qualify things, he may arrive at Truth by means of them. But if he continues to use them after they have ceased to represent anything in his mind, the result may be nonsense.

"If one man can do a piece of work in twelve hours, how long will it take two men to do it?" asks the teacher. Is a child permitted to bring his native common-sense into action and ask "What kind of work?" No indeed. He is taught to divide twelve by two. That two men will do a piece of work in half the time that it takes one man to do it is an absurd fallacy. If physical labor is meant, two men can do it in less than half the time; if mental labor, then one can work faster than two. One may work faster than a hundred.

It is the habit of statisticians to collect the figures that are attached to objects, separate them from the things to which they are attached, deal with them in various mysterious ways, then attach the results to the objects again and think that they have truth. A boy in a tree can pick six quarts of cherries in half an hour; then let the farmer borrow the services of his neighbor's daughter, and the boy and girl, so he is told, can pick six quarts of cherries in fifteen minutes. But any child knows that if you put a boy and a girl together in a tree they may not pick six quarts of cherries all day.

Mr. Wilbur Nesbit did a most excellent piece of figuring when he asserted that if a fox terrier two feet long, with a three-inch tail, could dig a hole four feet deep in half an hour, then to dig the Panama Canal in a single year would require only one fox terrier a mile and a half long, with an eighty-foot tail. Any statistician would gravely consider this statement, do a bit of figuring and assure you it is true; but a child would doubt it. He would question whether that kind of a fox terrier would dig where he was told.

It was once my pleasant fortune to be attached to a college for women (an attachment, may I add parenthetically, which in my heart still continues). In those days a statistician who lived in Pittsburgh, or some such place, announced that he had been making a study of the vital statistics of segregated colleges. He had discovered that the graduates of Vassar produced three-quarters of a child apiece, and the graduates of Harvard contributed to posterity only half a child per graduate. From this he deduced that such colleges not only were not reproducing themselves and must therefore cease to exist, but that they were a menace to civilization because they tended to reduce, generation by generation, the total number of educated people.

I was deeply interested in this; and my depraved fancy led me to wonder what grewsome fraction of an infant might come into the world if a graduate of Harvard married a graduate of Vassar. But as a more serious inquiry, I sought the source of his figures. I found that he worked with reports supplied by the colleges and obtained by "questionnaires" addressed to graduates. He had found the total number of graduates who had answered, and the total number of children that they had reported, and had conscientiously divided one figure by the other.

But a study of the letter-writing habits of college graduates, quite apart from any symbolic figures, reveals this interesting truth: that a young graduate who marries and acquires her first baby is very likely to write promptly to the alumnae secretary, or even wire the dean. When the second arrives, a belated postcard announces the fact. But after there are three or four in the family, the parent may forget to write at all. Moreover, such statistics are assembled from living graduates, seventy-five percent of whom are still physically able to bear more children. Such data would be of value only if it dealt with those alumni who have been out of college for forty years or more, or are dead.

But the statistician is interested in figures rather than human behavior. Having detached his symbols from living things, manipulated them, and then reattached them, he finds that such colleges must eventually disappear through failure to reproduce themselves. This is based on the assumption that all future students are produced only by former ones. Granting that absurdity, it would still be questionable whether such colleges menace our civilization. Common sense points out, on the contrary, that if Harvard and Vassar were cloistered spots, sending out trained graduates pledged to celibacy,

devoting their lives to teaching and social service, civilization still might benefit from their existence, or even
be more greatly benefited than at present.

I wrote to the gentleman in Pittsburgh, pointing out
some of the facts cited above, and added that my own
researches revealed that statisticians were producing a
quarter of a child apiece and that therefore in sixty
years or so there would be no more statisticians, for
which heaven be praised. I am still awaiting his reply.

Statisticians would do little harm if they avoided dis-
guises. The mere preparing of statistical tables, and the
riding up and down on graphs as though they were
roller coasters may keep them out of worse mischief.
But it is when the statistician calls himself an efficiency
expert that I most fear him. For then he takes his facts,
detaches them from reality, manipulates them, and attaches them again, with some sort of vested authority to
operate in human affairs. There is, for instance, the famous bricklayer and the stop watch. The efficiency expert observes the habits of the humble layer of bricks
and times his motions. He discovers that the man picks
up the brick, turns it over two or three times in his
hands in order to get the facing uppermost, spoons up
a little mortar with his trowel, perhaps even shifts his
implement and his brick from one hand to the other,
pauses to spit, and then puts the brick in place.

"If you will cut out three unnecessary motions," says the efficiency man, "you can lay twenty more bricks in an hour. If you can make your helper place the bricks in his hod with their faces up you can lay thirty more bricks in an hour." Figures are just as true in this instance as in the case of the fox terrier. How the bricklayer may feel when his behavior is thus mechanized is not the concern of the efficiency expert. How much a man *wants* to hurry with his work is not a ponderable force. It cannot be added or subtracted or multiplied into the equation. So forty bricklayers lay thirty more bricks apiece per hour, for one week, and go on strike at the beginning of the second week, because they want to pause and spit.

This is not a fanciful picture. At a certain canning factory a number of non-English-speaking women were employed at manual labor. Their employer had recently read about that converted bricklayer and was himself converted; so he sent for an efficiency engineer. First of all the factory was rearranged so that the several processes would be housed in logical order—the filled cans finally landing at the very doors of the freight cars. All that was well and good; the cans seemed to be as contented as ever, and production was increased.

But then the engineer began upon the lady Lithuanians. He studied their idiosyncrasies and found that some distinguished color more quickly than others, and some had quicker muscular reactions. So he jumped them about, until those who best distinguished colors selected labels for cans, and those whose feet moved most quickly operated foot-power machines, and so on. Then the wage was based upon a minimum output per individual, and a bonus offered for results in excess of that.

At the end of the first week a large number of these women earned a bonus and immediately struck. No one in the place could discover the reason; it was too subtle for the regular interpreter. But a priest was found in a neighboring city who spoke their tongue and he got at the root of the trouble. They had struck because they were overworked, but they did not know they were overworked until they were paid so much. The efficiency engineer departed in disgust. There was something there in addition to his figures which he could not add up.

Let this be credited to the teacher of elementary arithmetic, that he never urges a child to multiply six apples by two hippopotamuses in the belief that he will get twelve of either. Only a very stupid teacher would ask a child to divide, even on paper, one bone into six dogs and determine the fractional result, either in dogs or bones. He would fear a recrudescence of the child's common-sense, and a question as to the sizes of the various dogs. It is only after the teacher has become a statistician that he can subtract this year's white birth rate from this year's black birth rate, multiply by fifty years, and then frighten us with a rising tide of color.

I recall one such delver in digits who had spent years assembling figures relating to farm produce in a certain area. Finally he achieved his goal, which was to determine the average annual production. But by that time the inhabitants had begun raising something else.

Democracy is in most woeful need of all the expert theorists it can produce. It has bumbled along too far already without enough of them. In a monarchy or a despotism this is not the case (and if that be treason, make the most of it). Supreme authority scrutinizes its resources, discovers specialists in this or that, and summons them to the service of the state; and the populace does not resent this any more than other acts of omnipotence. On the contrary it is inclined to be boastful of its experts, making the same sort of fuss over them that it does over a royal family.

Certainly we democrats ought to have learned by this time what the expert theorist can do for us when we give him a chance. There is, for instance, a widespread belief that our bankers have been saved from final discredit by men who are pure theorists so far as banking is concerned. Insurance men once went through their own valley of the shadow, when they suddenly learned that the world had been changing around the insurance business, and it was necessary for a theorist to tell them about it.

Our railroads all prospered, as migratory peoples flowed in along their rights-of-way; and railroad executives, while cheerfully paralleling one another's lines, claimed credit, like Father Abraham, even for the populations, and for eighty years allowed an obsolete type of stage coach to determine the shape of a railway car, and custom to determine the price of a ticket. But at last when populations stopped flowing and business fell off they welcomed the counsel of theorists.

But it is more tactful of me to write about farmers. They are thick-skinned fellows who do not mind being written about. Several years ago an elderly theorist retired to his estate in an eastern farming section. He was depressed by the depleted soil and inferior stock and antiquated methods of his farmer neighbors, and eagerly desired to be of practical use to them. He suggested the introduction of another breed of cattle as best suited to their hillsides; and certain European tricks of viniculture that promised better results. But they would have none of him. Finally his farm manager, who was a native and knew his own people, suggested building a good fence around everything, and following a policy of extreme reticence. The plan worked. Neighbors climbed the fence by night and borrowed the ideas, as well as a little breeding from the foreign stock. The whole neighborhood was greatly benefited, and every farmer felt that it was a result of his own rugged individualism. Experts be durned.

I met a young stage driver in South Dakota who pointed across the distant prairies to his home farm, and I asked why he had not followed in his father's footsteps. "Because farmers haven't any sense," he answered. "Even after the state granted tree claims, you couldn't get some of these farmers to plant trees. They never had planted trees before and why should they now? Wheat was what they planted, and they knew all they needed to know about that. When the state offered to give a squatter full title to a piece of land if he would plant trees and stay until they had grown into a storm barrier, a few outsiders came in and took advantage of the offer. But my dad never would, and he's had all his savings swept away twice by wind storms.

"Take pigs," continued the lad. "When I was a youngster we always kept one family of pigs around the back door. They used up the family swill and we killed them when they got big enough. One family of pigs was enough for one farmhouse. We knew they would thrive in this climate, but that didn't suggest anything to a farmer. All he could see was wheat. It took some crazy expert from the state college to pound into the farmers' heads the idea that they might raise more pigs, and they resisted the idea as long as they could. Now a big part of the state's wealth is pork products."

It looks as though democracy might get along better if the specialist and the practical man of affairs could work together in hearty coöperation, each supplementing the other. This might happen if any one of the following conditions could be brought about: first, if every practical man of affairs were also a specialist; second, if every specialist were a practical man of affairs; third, if we could train up a trusted and trustworthy body of interpreters.

The first condition will come about when every citizen is possessed of so thorough a knowledge in some one field that, with the humility of the true scholar, he respects the learning of others. This presupposes universal education, and the millennium.

The second might come about if we could pass laws requiring every specialist to spend three days of every week in general reading or mingling with his fellow men and striving to understand them. This seems equally difficult!

The third condition is a matter for the press. The newspaperman is our interpreter. If our experiment in democracy is to work, we must be able to count on his integrity, high purpose and good sense.

Unfortunately, the newspaperman has become, to a considerable extent, merely a dealer in a commodity called Sensation. Instead of helping the expert to explain his profound discoveries to common men, he persuades him to say something silly, and gives that to the world in letters an inch high. He teaches wise men to distrust newspapers and the public to distrust wise men. He might save experts for democracy; he might, and should, save democracy for itself.

XI

Reincarnation

THERE have come moments, after I have been contemplating the social behavior of myself and my kind, when I hope that the animals do not form judgments upon man. The dictum of our puny science, that animals do not think, is a sort of protective reaction. We do not want them to think, because we do not like to think what they might be thinking about us.

In some of their social arrangements they have notably excelled us. An ant hill is so much more orderly than one of our cities; a beaver colony so much more efficient.

Yet they too are handicapped just as we are, by variations in the individual. They have their drones and their annoying examples of energy, their gay and their morose, their taciturn and their loud-mouthed. All of these must somehow learn to live together in a hill or behind a dam.

Any one who sees much of these lower creatures

must occasionally amuse himself, as I have, in picking out the prototypes of his friends and acquaintances. After a summer spent among horses and cattle, I find myself wondering whether the doctrine of reincarnation is not after all worthy of acceptance. At any rate, there is pleasure to be had from playing with it.

Skinny little dogs, for instance: they are the reincarnated souls of men who always knew at any given time just what was wrong with the government. When anything is afoot they yap. If they hear a fracas two backyards away, they are vociferous. If it is in the next yard, they are exclamatorily indignant. If it comes into their own yard, they hide and yap afterward. They hate foreigners, and distrust all strangers. All privileges they ever enjoyed they claim as rights. They can neither demand with courtesy nor obey with grace. But they can always yap and yap.

June-bugs are the souls of certain ladies who in life loved summer hotel verandas. They haunt all brightly lighted porch rockers; but the dark attracts them because they know that something improper must be going on in it. They are ever curious, and peer into lighted windows but are doomed to bump their noses against the panes. As humans it was hard to be rid of them, so now they are sticky, and cling. And incessantly they buzz and flutter and buzz.

Cicadas are the souls of those clergymen and other orators who in lifetime always know positively just what God thinks and what He intends to do. They perch in high places and say nothing new, but are terribly reiterative. Just about every seventeen years they join their voices in an asseverating chorus that drowns out the quiet speculative chirpings of humbler insects.

XII

Joiners

ON pleasant mornings a little group of dogs assembles on the street corner just to the west of us and, after the roll has been called and rituals observed, trots eastward in a leisurely but purposeful manner, gathering up our dog on the way. Perhaps not every pleasant morning; but stated meetings occur at least every Wednesday and Saturday, while adjourned conclaves or executive committees assemble with more whimsical irregularity.

I have often wondered what might be the qualifications for membership in that group. The rites they observe are no more Scottish than they are Irish or Welsh or mongolian. Obviously there is no flaunting of a common ancestry. They are not Descendants of Somebody or Something. Yet there must be definite exclusions, since some of the neighborhood dogs do not qualify. At every meeting I note that the order of business includes the consideration of new members, rejection of applicants usually being carried by acclaim, with prompt action by hastily appointed officials.

A little way up the street there lives a small dog who does not belong. Probably he never applied, for I know that the membership is composed of his personal friends. But he sits upon the terrace in front of his house and barks at the organization as it trots past him, bent upon its business. If, as I surmise, there is no sharp criticism implied in his bark, but merely an amused and friendly tolerance, then that little dog might well be I.

For among the shortcomings of my riper years is a lack of that widespread human urge to join something. Though I love the beat of a drum, I do not want to put on a red fez and blue sash and, in time with a hundred other fezzes and sashes, measure my own footfalls by its throbbing. My spirit warms to an inner glow whenever I tell my children some legend of the *Mayflower* or the *Ann,* of Louisburg or Yorktown or the covered wagons. But it does not warm toward an assemblage of males or females of my kind, brought together only because they are competent to pass similar legends along to their own young. I like to lunch in the company of my fellow-men—even to raise my voice with theirs in song; but not at stated intervals, under compulsion.

All of this is a humble confession, and not a boast.

Joining is undoubtedly one of the primitive impulses; and the older a man gets the less he courts the suspicion that he lacks any primal urge. A sophistication which wars with nature is flaunted only by the young or the decrepit; and at this moment of writing I am neither. There may, however, be something the matter with my red or my white corpuscles which keeps them from assembling or drawing apart as they should; or some as yet unchristened gland may have dropped out at a time when I was undergoing repairs.

Certain it is that in my youth I joined everything that would admit me, from Christian Endeavor to the Schiller Street Gang. I can still recall an Agassiz Society, a fife-and-drum corps, an electric club, at least three literary-and-debating societies, a missionary circle, and successive groups which collected stamps, camped out, broke windows, danced-and-ate, or just danced, or just ate. Or perhaps I am a proof that the human Urge-to-Join is something which can burn out. Mine, I suspect, flared up and died with Atlantic Hook, Hose, and Ladder Company No. 1. Such joining as I have done since that has been due to social compulsion rather than to inner urge.

Even among the lower animals it seems to be possible for the impulse to abate, though I am told that the lower the animal the less likely is this to occur. I

recall an old beaver on a pond in Maine who had with-
drawn from the local organization, and insisted upon
building a private dam of his own. There are occasional
wild geese which refuse to join any of the many
V-shaped formations flying south, because they prefer
to travel alone. Now and then a crow is observed who
will not unite with the local debating society but goes
off somewhere to caw by himself. Very, very infre-
quently a non-joiner has been noted among the monkeys. And then there is that little dog up our street.

A friendly psychologist tells me—and he always
speaks as though he knew—that those animals which
first happened to group themselves into mutual protective associations survived, and those which did not,
perished; and this continued until social grouping became a fixed habit with certain species. To join became
an instinct and not a matter of individual choice. So
far have the Behaviorists carried these researches that
I find it difficult to follow them, especially since I
speak only their last year's vernacular; and so completely do they seem to have become *en rapport* with
the dumber animals that it is difficult at times for me
to tell one from the other.

I think it is Von Nirgend who develops most richly
the details of lower-animal social organization. Lack of
space prevents me from quoting any complete sentence;

and he is especially hard to follow because of his tendency to force his verbs over into the appendix of his book. But he has closely studied the widely prevalent custom among animal groups of selecting one member to stand guard while the others argue or eat; and this he holds to be the earliest development in the direction of club life. His studies have led him to conclude that this important sentinel position in the group was elective and not appointive; in fact, he is inclined to believe that this and the leadership, or presidency, still constitute the only two flock and herd offices. In a copious footnote he asserts that the sole barrier to a more elaborate club life among the lower animals has been their inability to record by-laws and the minutes of preceding meetings; and he directly traces to this primitive heritage the British contentment with an unwritten constitution.

Such research, even when thus sketchily followed, is stimulating to the lay imagination. I am bold enough to disagree with Von Nirgend when he hints that in the sentry of the animal flock we find the germ idea of the human sergeant-at-arms. Such a deduction is superficial and over-obvious. This sentry position was too important. It carried with it authority over the leader himself. These sentinels were so placed as to command a wider view of outside affairs, and their orders, even though communicated through the leader or president as a matter of form, were meekly obeyed by the entire herd. It seems obvious to me that we have here the earliest suggestion of an executive-secretary-ship.

Though we higher animals are bound to join something as a matter of instinct,* our complicated social structure, and the limited number of meeting days in a month, compel us to exercise some intelligence, no matter how little, in deciding which things to join. Von Nirgend points out a fundamental distinction between the grouping habits of the lower and the higher animals. This impulse among the birds and beasts first arose from a desire for companionship and mutual protection. But human beings, in making the choice of a group, first consider those who are not in it. In other words, we must know who is excluded before we will join. The men marching up the street in fezzed ranks are not stimulated so much by an affection for their fellow-marchers as by a comfortable sense of superiority over the unfezzed multitude on the sidewalk.

This principle is clearly illustrated by the ancestral societies. No Son or Daughter of Something-or-Other ever joined the society because of a love for the con-

---

* I am told that "instinct" is a word belonging to the vernacular of year before last, and has been replaced by a longer word meaning much the same thing.

temporary membership. If such an affection played any small part in his decision it was dissipated the moment he first viewed an assemblage of his fellow-members. Loyalty to these groups is based upon a consideration of those who are excluded. The more shut out, the greater the loyalty of those in, and the more apply for admittance. An elusive memory flickers through my mind of an American society of Descendants which found itself excluding so small a number of fellow-citizens that the membership became discontented, and a second hive of Sons swarmed, with articles so drawn that more were excluded. Then things went much better.

When one notes this basic principle underlying our joining impulse it is easier to understand why the Daughters of the American Revolution have gone on record as opposed to any further revolutions of any sort. One revolution on the national record provides its daughters with hardly enough exclusiveness; but a second revolution, with the population as large as it is now, would make things very difficult for the Daughters' daughters. One could hardly draw the line anywhere.

Ancestral societies are generally fortunate in that so few of their members delve into mathematics. I know, for instance, that I must have had four grandparents and eight great-grandparents, and that the least lovable of my fellow-citizens could have had no less. I must, therefore, have had more than a thousand of them in the single generation when our first immigrants were landing; and if only I knew who they all were I should be able to join almost anything. During the period loosely described as that of the Colonial Wars I had more than seventeen hundred grandparents living and, considering the colonial census of that day, some of them must have been up to something. But it is regrettably true that our plumber, a native American whom I dislike, had just as many, and regrettably probable that he may rightfully claim some of mine.

I have heard of a society made up of the descendants of the barons who signed the great charter at Runnymede. A little calculating shows that one baron of that day, who had three children, with each child having three, and so on down the generations, would today have 265,890,889,094,649 descendants. Allowing for wars, pestilences, and several barren barons, one might still claim a right to membership in that society without bothering to search the records.

Ancestry is, in fact, the least discriminating of all methods of exclusion. Genealogical research is a fascinating study to those who have the time for it, but honestly pursued it should make for humility. It is no respecter of persons. Genealogical volumes in any well conducted library might well be classified as satire. *Life,* in an editorial many years ago, pointed out this fundamental weakness in ancestral societies, and urged for the sake of real exclusiveness the establishment of one made up of the Descendants of the Spinster Aunts of Reigning Sovereigns.

If the universality of this human Urge-to-Join were more generally recognized there might be less artificial pressure upon the young to start societies and "movements." Although Age is forever urging Youth to curb one impulse or another, in this particular Age reverses its custom. A surprising number of clubs, societies, and organizations for the young are planned by adults, and youths are all too easily herded into them. Generally the objects of these groups are adult purposes thinly disguised.

The old-fashioned Sunday-school notably illustrates this. A child caught in its toils was encouraged to join societies, guilds, bands, circles, little brothers, little sisters, and troops without number, each of them having presidents, vice presidents, secretaries and treasurers, by-laws, badges, and minutes of preceding meetings— and all devised by adults. Wherever youth is assembled in any numbers there you may be sure the organizing adult is getting in his work. The average university campus is honeycombed by his burrowings. "Honorary" societies, owing their vitality not to their inclusive but to their exclusive character, are so multiplied that I have known of sixty within a single university. Youth needs no encouragement in this direction, yet most of these organizations were instigated and are encouraged by the enthusiasm of older folk, some of whom, I regret to say, are sustained as "general officers" by a share of youth's annual dues.

In every section of our country can be found earnest-minded adults who feel that America should have a "youth movement"; with the result that here and there small groups of youths are constantly being persuaded to move, with a president, three vice presidents, two secretaries, and by-laws. But the difficulty lies in keeping them going after the members discover that anybody may join. This whole business of a youth movement would be easier if only we could draw a more sharply dividing line between age and youth. But it grows steadily harder as grandmothers experiment with cosmetics and insist upon going out to dance.

There is really very little that we can do about a primal urge. But at least I can complain, or even lodge a protest with the executive committee, when I see it being over-encouraged or badly misdirected. The average human being joins a society because he is obeying an instinct and, except for settling the question of which to join, without the exercise of any thought. After he is a member, he never thinks of Thinking as in any way associated with club life. When it comes to the drawing up of resolutions or other intellectual effort by the group as a whole, he leaves it to the secretary. As this habit grows, association members get to thinking less and less, and their executive secretaries more and more.

After all, a good executive secretary must earn his salary. It is his business to think of all the things that his association ought to be thinking, then obtain their acquiescence by stamped and self-addressed envelope, and proceed to draw up resolutions or write to a senate committee. A truly energetic executive secretary gets to thinking that whatever he thinks is, and of a right ought to be, the majority opinion of his organization, so he acts immediately without waiting to find out. He is the sort of man who Gets Things Done; and he is well worth whatever any society is able to pay him.

A short time ago in a smoking car I had an interesting chat which bears upon this very point. My seat-companion proved to be a manufacturer of mousetraps, and at that time president of the American Association of Mousetrap Manufacturers. I found him a friendly and confiding soul, devoted to his family and highly conscientious in his business. It seems he had been reared from earliest infancy in the belief that if he made a better mousetrap the world would find a way to his door.

"You do not believe in a protective tariff?" I asked in surprise, after some political comment of his.

"No, indeed," he replied. "I am sure that international trade will always make a pathway—" he cleared his throat—"find channels—"

"But," said I, "here is an item to the effect that your association has demanded a high duty on foreign traps, and reciprocal arrangements on cheese."

He glanced hurriedly at my paper. "Yes, yes," he said nervously, "I—we—feel very strongly—" his eyes wandered. "We have an excellent executive secretary," he murmured. "Evans is the sort of man who gets things done."

One wonders how many letters reach Washington every day signed "Executive Secretary," and how many more composed by him and signed by somebody else. Any senator any day may find in his mail the type of letter which reads: "The National Association of Safety-Pin Manufacturers, representing more than two hundred executives and more than two thousand office

clerks and skilled laborers who are intelligently loyal
to the interests of their employers, notes with alarm
your attitude toward zippers—etc., etc. Signed, Executive Secretary for the Nat. Assn. of S. P. Mfrs." Yet it
is quite possible that eighty per cent of the members
of that association, and ninety per cent of its employees
never noted with alarm or any other emotion anything
the senator ever said. It is even possible that many of
the members are deriving personal satisfaction from the
use of zippers for one purpose or another, and would
warmly endorse the senator's views.

When following this line of thought a hopeful be-
liever in democracy must thank God all over again for
the institution of the secret ballot. It is this impulse to
join, more than anything else, which makes us so
amenable to bosses, political leaders, and executive secretaries. The astute politician turns his party organization into a club, with a president, vice president,
secretary, and treasurer, and a meeting place where
billiard and bridge tournaments and corn roasts are the
order of business rather than political discussion. Such
a club authorizes the secretary to cast a single ballot
on all political questions.

Common sense is an individual and not a collective
possession, and without the secret ballot it would have
small chance to assert itself. No class of our citizenship

is free from that impelling desire to assemble into small excluding flocks and herds; and only the final sacred moment of solitary confinement in a canvas booth ever saves the best of us from being voted in batches. Even that does not save us very often.

As to cultural levels, I suspect that the joining impulse enjoys its greatest debauch in what we are pleased to call the upper stratum of our society. It is reasonable that this should be so, if one joins in order to exclude. For it is on such levels that the greatest value is placed upon exclusiveness. It is easier, for instance, to vote an organization of railroad presidents as though they were one man than an organization of their employees. This is heresy; but I have borrowed the idea from a railroad executive who believes that one of the emptiest threats of our every-day politics is the boast of the labor leader that he can deliver the vote *en bloc* of any intelligent labor group. After all the buncome and the ballyhoo, such men are more inclined to walk into the booth and vote according to individual preference than are their employers, who cherish an even stronger sense of clan membership. Why not? That consciousness is sustained by the fact that within their own stratum each may be paying dues to a dozen clubs and societies which constantly remind him of the clan obligation and the class point of view.

These be witch-hunting days, and many prophets are foretelling the collapse of our political structure, and the rise of naziism, bolshevism, collectivism, or other isms too dangerous to name above a whisper. Societies are being formed for the sole purpose of discovering and curtailing the activities of other societies. Why then is some one not organizing us against that imminent menace, executive-secretarianism? Doubtless the danger is more difficult to see and define because we are now in the midst of it. This is already a government of the people, for clubs, societies and associations, by executive secretaries. Even now it may be perishing from the earth.

I have an important notion, as yet only half formed, that we might do much toward balancing our national budget if we could only deflect the mighty stream of initiation fees and annual dues into the nation's treasury. There would be little economic and no social danger attending taxation of this sort, because you cannot tax a primal urge out of existence. Citizens would be far readier to limit themselves in the matter of smoking, or of raising more pigs, than to deny themselves the joy of joining something. The stream would continue to flow in almost undiminished volume.

If this suggestion arouses indignant protest—as it undoubtedly might—I have an alternative to propose. We might profitably do away with a vast number of our present organizations if we could only harness up man's joining impulse to the idea of joining the Human Race. Undoubtedly we could "sell" this idea generally if we could somehow formalize the business. There would have to be a minimum age limit—with a junior membership, of course—and some forms of initiation ceremony, ritual, and insignia. As to the latter, many ideas suggest themselves. There should be heraldic quarterings, to include a hint of common ancestry, and devices symbolic of sin and salvation. Perhaps we could not avoid the bar sinister; for we must frankly admit that unless some such episode occurred in our record we should all still be monkeys.

If we are to make the plan attractive it will be necessary to emphasize exclusiveness; but I am sure we could agree to exclude anthropoids and possibly all surviving bushmen. I should like to add all professional organizers (call this professional jealousy, if you like), also census enumerators, statisticians, psychologists, and others whose business or avocation it is to stand on the outside looking in. Just between ourselves, I should like to add radio crooners and several individuals, including Aimee Semple McPherson. If we could once get this organization going, it might do much toward the bringing about of international peace. But we must be wary of executive secretaries—especially the sort of man who Gets Things Done.

XIII

A Worm's Turning

OLD MOTHER NATURE, I suspect, is the one who smiles most broadly at the human race, amused at man's extravagant claims to superiority over the lower animals. I wonder whoever first bestowed upon her that saintly appellation? Obviously, it was not I. Not only is she never old, but she is a frivolous creature, a player of practical jokes, a mischief maker. Just when a man is most pompous or profound or condescending, along comes Nature and lays her delicate fingers upon his arm, or perhaps gives him no more than a glance, and lo! he is stripped of all his pretenses.

Looking back, I can recall a hundred times when she has upset the structure of a dignity which I had been at great pains to build. Let me but assume a lofty manner, or otherwise adjust myself to some stately company, and along comes Nature, laughing in my face and tearing off all the surface of my conceit.

But I can be goaded just so far and no farther. I shall

turn the tables and tell what I know. I have been spying upon the lady to some purpose, and since she has shown that she will not let me alone, she may take the consequences.

For I have discovered that she has four lovers. When first I surprised her, after my eyes were opened, she was posing as a shy demure creature, eyes downcast, dark lashes almost hiding her sparkling glance. She was clad in quiet brown, set off alluringly with delicate shades of green. Spring was wooing her, and so cool and retiring was she, that butter would not melt in her mouth. Yet I noted her sly advances; so, smiling to myself, I left them, knowing full well the course events would take.

Even with my suspicions thus aroused I was not ready for what followed. For of a sudden I came upon her folded in the arms of Summer. Gone was all her shyness and demure manner. She was lush and bold and unwithholding. She was tropical in her abandon, so that I was embarrassed; and I slipped away, wondering at her inconstancy.

Time passed, and though I knew what I knew, I said nothing. Then I came upon her again, and this time I had no question about her. For she had clothed herself in such garments as I had never seen her in before. Decked from head to foot in brilliant red and gold, she had obviously set out upon another conquest. Gone was the maidenly manner; vanished her languishment of surrender. Now she was stately, brilliant, sophisticate; and I pitied the poor dupe, whoever he was, who might attempt to withstand her wiles and her beauty.

Brazen as I now knew her to be, I could find it in my heart to pity her for the climax that she brought upon herself. Until now it had plainly been she who made all the advances, working her own shameless will by her various devices. And then the catastrophe! I had come suddenly to the place where she had just been standing. There were her garments, strewn all about,—bits of torn finery, broken baubles, crushed blossoms, even dainty hairpins scattered under foot. Then suddenly I saw them as they hurried past. He had thrown a white sheet about her, and from his encircling arm I could see that there was no escape. But as they passed I noted the flashing excitement in her eyes,—and I could swear she liked it!

Nature has shamed me once too often. I know I am taking risks, because the fact is that she knows entirely too many things about me. Nevertheless, I am now telling the truth about her. Nature is a strumpet,—a shameless huzzy.

XIV

The Inferiority of Inferior Animals

I ONCE had a small dog, and you must listen to a story about him. If you too have a dog, you will bear with me, because you will be patiently waiting to get an anecdote of your own in edgewise.

His name was Dundee. He was a West Highland terrier, but at the time this incident occurred he was well past puppyhood and the gentleness and dignity which had been his since birth had grown with the years. He seldom barked; and romped only under extreme provocation. His chief characteristic was quiet devotion to his human friends.

My wife and daughter and I had taken him with us into the southwest, and on this particular afternoon had started our car across the wasteland of the Navajo reservation toward Shiprock, hoping to reach the foot of it before dark. But roads dwindled into trails and trails died in arroyos and darkness settled down before we reached our destination. So we decided to spend the warm night just where we were, on car cushions and blankets. A brilliant moon came up, providing an eerie sort of daylight. When it left us, real darkness came with the vast black shadow of the rock against the stars, and a spooky sort of silence that was intensified by desert sounds. A little fire of dry sage flared up as we fed it, and died down quickly. Just as we were really trying to sleep the silence was shattered by the bark of coyotes. There is a wicked sound to their laughter. You cannot tell just where it comes from, or how far away it is; and I think that we all were a little affected by the sound. Then suddenly the wailing, snarling bark sounded close by. There was no questioning its nearness, though I had supposed that a coyote would not dare to come so close. I picked up a bit of stone and stole on tiptoe toward the sound. Just over a little rise, I came upon Dundee. There he sat facing the black night and the direction from which the wild voices had come. He had just raised his muzzle and begun another answering wail so exactly like the cry of the wild pack that at a distance you could not distinguish between them. My appearance stopped him short. His muzzle came down, and he came waggling toward me, his tail between his legs, his whole manner indicating shame. Together we returned to the car, and I offered him no word of reproach. Civilized little house pet that he was, he had had his moment, and I would not disturb his memory of it.

I am moved to further anecdote. Dundee had short legs and could not make speed under the best of conditions. In the snow, he was pathetic. Running on low, the two back cylinders had difficulty in firing. On his daily walk with me across a certain pleasant campus he often saw a squirrel and with undying optimism pursued it to the nearest tree and then with his eyes followed it into the highest branches.

One winter day we took our walk through a light fall of snow. It was not deep enough to hamper his going, so when a squirrel crossed his path, he actually overtook it at the base of a tree. Nothing in his experience provided for such an emergency. His excitement was intense. I think the squirrel's fur actually tickled his nose as it ran up the tree trunk. I had to go the rest of the way without him on that particular morning, and I am told that he sat by that tree for hours while his nerves calmed down.

The point is this: he never seemed to forget the adventure; but for months after, whenever we came to that point in our morning walk, he would look excitedly around for another squirrel, and then dash for the same old tree.

"He remembered all about it a year later," I said

when telling a psychologist friend. "He is forever hoping that he will overtake another squirrel; and this time he imagines he will know what to do."

" 'Remembering!' " said my friend, " 'hoping,' 'suspecting,' 'imagining!' People are always using these words about animals. Your little dog did not think; he did not 'remember,' in your sense of the word. He does not 'hope' or 'suspect.' A certain experience cut a deep mark on the surface of his brain, to phrase the thing so that you will understand it, and now, when certain associations repeat themselves, automatic reaction leads him to repeat some of the physical maneuvers of that former day."

"Ah!" said I. Then I told my learned friend about the horse that I found sympathetically licking the back of a pig which had caught its tusks in a wire fence and was shrieking with agony.

" 'Sympathetically,'—that is a word you have no right to use. One animal does not feel sympathy for another."

"How do you know?"

"That is rather a large question for the moment we have at our disposal," said my friend, with a hint of condescension. "It would carry us into behaviorism and back into a good many of the elementary processes of psychology, if I answered it in a fashion you would understand."

"And all this while," I said, "what do you suppose a horse thinks about you?"

"Absolutely nothing," said my friend coldly.

"Well that, at least, indicates common sense," I retorted, and our little discussion ended.

Surely there is no false humility in me when, in moments of fancy, I think of horses as my equals. One pictures them pacing, single-footing, trotting, galloping down through the ages. They go with man into battle; they carry messages from Ghent to Aix; they breast swollen rivers; they form barriers of their bodies to protect man from an enemy's bullets, giving their lives for his; they pace riderless but fully caparisoned beside the biers of dead heroes.

Man moiled along slowly upward through the centuries toward civilization on his own two feeble legs, until he found this friend to carry him faster and more tirelessly on four.

What annoys me most about the argument against the thinking of animals is that precisely the same arguments may be used to prove that human beings do not think. We too experience certain inevitable reactions. Some of my psychologist friends say, "You are quite right; the processes are the same." That is what I want them to say. For then I can throw away all the old terminology and declare,—"whatever it is we humans do, my friend the horse does it also. He hopes; he fears; he loves; he distrusts; he envies; he hates; he reasons that certain procedures are wiser or more practical than others. If there are other words for all of these things, I am willing to use them, as long as we both know what we are talking about."

" 'Reasoning,' " says my friend, "that is too much! 'Intuition' is the word you want there."

All right. I am content with intuition. I saw a boy working out an intricate mathematical problem with his sister. Suddenly she said, "I am sure I have the answer!"

"You couldn't possibly have it," he retorted. "You haven't had time to work it out."

"I didn't work it out," she replied. "All of a sudden I knew it."

He looked at me aggrievedly. "She's always doing that," he said. "It's very annoying."

I have a friend in the west who loves horses. "Do they think?" he said. "Of course they think! Ride behind a herd on a cow pony whose duty it is to head off stragglers. You do not need to use the rein. If a steer breaks away and starts at right angles from the line of march through the brush, your pony will adopt the course that will best head him off. Inevitably he starts at the proper angle, and never directly in pursuit. Let another steer break away in a different sort of terrain and at a different speed; the pony gages speed, and angle, and character of the land, and heads him off with the least waste of energy. Call it instinct if you like. I do not care what you call it, so long as you will remember that that horse never chased that cow in that place before."

My friend, who is a kindly philosopher, believes that human wisdom is but a fragment of the whole truth, and Truth is another name for God. All living creatures are endowed with means for acquiring their own little fragment of that God-head. The man who allows his power of perception to become dulled weakens his power to gain truth. Men of differing perceptions gain different fragments, and it is not for one to say that the other's portion is better than his own.

If I can study nature with a deeply discerning eyesight; learn to tell the mosses by my finger tips; distinguish mushrooms by their faint aromas; gradually by these means I move in the direction of infinity of knowledge, which is complete truth, or eternal blessedness, or Heaven, or any of the other good old names for it.

What does a horse see when he looks down the wind? What sense tells him of an approaching storm? What can a dog learn from the scent on a blade of grass washed by three rains? And when these creatures have not only kept the keenness of sense-perception with which they were endowed, but have intensified it by use rather than squandered it by abuse, how can man say what smaller portion of wisdom is theirs, gained through skills in which he is a mere bungler?

A wise man tells me that animals have no morals,— only manners. Manners are so often the outward evidence of morality, we are led to assume, in the case of a "mannerly" animal, that morals lie beneath the surface. But these polite ways are merely habits of behavior that have been drilled into him, and arise from no inward state of grace.

Morals or not, I am content to believe that not only does my horse think, but that he is quite as likely to earn a place in heaven as I am. If we are both dependent upon the brain convolutions formed by our ancestors, we must have many instincts in common; for when man was living in a cave a million years ago, as some of our wise men assert, or fifty million years ago, as others insist, the little eohippus was his friend. While our scientists are groping back through that darkness of antiquity to find when man began, with less trouble they have been tracing the horse as far back, or further.

It is amusing to think that this steed which eyes me

through drooping eyelids, reflectively, half sleepily, but instant to note my every motion, may be calmly aware of his more ancient lineage, and conscious of an inherited guardianship. *Noblesse oblige!* Though I spur him, yet will he carry me.

XV

Manners and Morals

FROM what do human manners arise, most excellent Theophilus? Are they related in any way to morals? If as a teacher I should urge good manners upon my students, which manners should I urge? Is it always and everywhere good manners for a man to remove his hat in church? Ask the Quakers. Or bad manners to remove one's shoes when out calling? Ask the Japanese. Business men have not yet decided whether an elevator is part of the entrance to a building or an inside room. Some polite men remove their hats when a lady enters, and some do not. A polite Chinese practices the knack of belching at the dinner table of his host; he has eaten more than he ought, the food is so delicious. In our polite circles, we practice the avoidance of it.

When new social conditions arise, we have to think up a new set of manners. For instance, we have not yet formulated good manners for the telephone. A polite man who would never think of pushing rudely ahead of others while waiting at the doctor's office, will step out of the line, go down to the corner drugstore, telephone the doctor and get in ahead of all the rest. And the doctor does not know how to avoid such an interruption.

It is generally impolite to interrupt, but a telephone interrupts anybody, any time, anywhere, without censure. When polite people come to feel that a telephone is an extension of the manners of the person who is using it, then will come a code. After that, television will come, and what had become telephone politeness may find itself impolite.

When moral standards change, a new set of manners is needed. For manners are the outside signals we fly to announce that certain morals exist inside us. Occasionally these codes are changed by common agreement, and folk in another generation, who have not heard about the change, misread the signals. It is not true today that a lady flaunting a cigarette in public is signaling her lack of virtue; but there are still elderly people alive who have not learned that this signal has changed.

The manners of Christendom are the small indications that the comfort of my neighbor is my first consideration. I walk at the outside, when going along the street with a woman, because her safety is more important to me than my own. As street dangers decrease, the basis in morals ceases to exist, but the manner continues for a time, because the code has not yet been changed by common consent. Among tribes which hold a religious belief demanding death to all enemies it is good morals to stab an enemy in the back, and good manners to go about with splashes of gore on the face. Even after the belief is dead, the facial adornment may for a little time continue to be *au fait*.

Manners are the children of morals, and the grandchildren of religious convictions; and they may live on, after their parents are dead and buried. One may even by imitation acquire manners without the morals back of them, and make community living pleasanter for everybody.

But if I must choose which manners I shall teach, I should say those whose parents are still living.

XVI

Hospitality

CONSIDER Hospitality, for instance. With the Greeks it was a matter of morals; with us it is merely manners. The Greeks had a word for it,—*euxenos*—and what is more they knew just what the word meant and all that it might mean. Yet unreasonably enough we borrowed our own word from the Latin,—*hospitalitas*—and then it took us a long time to work it over into current usage.

The Greeks (who knew how to tell stories to adults so simply that children might enjoy them) deemed hospitality the greatest of the virtues. Thus it is that we moderns, who rate it as an outer garment to be donned or doffed for convenience's sake, cannot read the story of *Alcestis* with complete appreciation. Here is the gist of it.

Admetus and his wife were young and intensely devoted to the business of loving one another. But the fates had decreed that Admetus should die. Then comes Apollo, after the intriguing fashion of those old Greek

gods who were forever messing into human affairs, and
argues with Death about it. Death claims his due, but
is willing to accept a substitute. Admetus discusses the
matter with his aged parents, who presumably have
not many more years to live. But they do not view his
proposition favorably. In fact the old gentleman gets
rather nasty about it. Then it is that young Mrs.
Admetus offers herself for the sacrifice and her husband
agrees.

Most of this is told to us in advance by an obliging
chorus, and the action begins in a house of mourning
where a despairing young man weeps over the body of
his love and realizes what a despicable egoistic wretch
he has been. Incidentally old Admetus Senior says nothing to comfort him.

Then comes the guest, a big roystering chap with a
letter of introduction, Hercules by name; and the law
of hospitality dominates that house. It is true, admits
the young host, there has been a death here; a servant,
a stranger; do not let that mar the joy of your visit.
So, with the death chamber shut off, and Admetus trying likewise to shut the door of his heart upon his bitter
grief, the visitor is entertained according to his bent.
There is wining and dining, dancing and riotous play
in the guest's chambers, with drunken complaints now
and then from Hercules that his host seems not to enter

whole-heartedly into the fun. Then Admetus slips away for the funeral, and a grief-stricken servant who had been left at home to care for the guest lets the truth leak out. With the shock of it, Hercules sobers up. Great is his shame for his own conduct; greater still his sorrow that the lady of that house is dead; but greatest of all his admiration for Admetus who could so nobly uphold the law of hospitality; for the comfort and happiness of the guest has transcended all other considerations. Thus it is that Hercules in expiation is moved to seek Death in his sunless home, struggle with him, and rescue the dead wife.

"I trust that I shall bring up Alcestis," he soliloquizes, "so as to place her in the hands of that host who received me into his house, nor drove me away although struck with a heavy calamity, but concealed it, noble as he was, having respect unto me. Who of the Thessalians is more hospitable than he?"

The dramatic moment of the play arrives when Hercules brings a shrouded figure into the presence of the grieving Admetus and demands that as a last act of consideration for a guest's whims he shall take this strange woman into his home in place of the wife who is dead. And so the play closes happily with these lines in the final speech:

"But lead her in, Admetus, and as thou oughtest

henceforward, continue in piety with respect to strangers."

Then there was the case of Procrustes. The Greeks have told us about him, being careful to mention at the same time that he was not a Greek; probably of some mixed breed with a strain of Persian in him. His first name seems not to be a matter of record, but it might easily have been Georgos or Michel. This Mike Procrustes had a large place set well back from the road on the main highway from Eleusis to Athens. In fact it was about half way, and so far from either point that motorists were likely to be out of gas or in need of a night's lodging when they reached the entrance of the estate. George had a few of his retainers planted casually near the highway with instructions to invite any belated travelers in for refreshment and a night's lodging. If they were Greeks, they were not surprised at this, since such hospitality to strangers was taken for granted.

But Procrustes seems to have been a degenerate of some sort, with sadistic tendencies. He had a guest-room bed which was his particular pride. One guest after another was invited to occupy that bed, and then carried to it, hog-tied. If he happened not to fit it exactly, the head butcher and his assistants stood ready. The guest was lopped off if he proved to be too long and stretched out if he proved to be too short,—and few survived the ordeal. George M. Procrustes seems to have kept up this playful business until Theseus, who was a sort of state constabulary complete in one person, happened along that way and made Procrustes sleep in his own spare bedroom.

So there we have in revealing fable the opposite extremes of hospitality,—the Greek and the barbarian. Reviewing a life-time of my own experiences as a guest, I am not quite certain which extreme I prefer. For there have been good Greek ladies who were, I am sure, hiding dire catastrophe while they made me welcome. Subdued telephone conversations, inevitably overheard, make it clear that some cherished plan has been abandoned; at dinner I am assured, after intercepting a wig-wag eyebrow semaphore, that Edward always skips the squab; and the appearance of the library at breakfast time is obvious proof that Susanne has slept on the sofa. "She likes to," insists the hostess; "she often does it when there is no one here."

Yet I had not been permitted to refuse the invitation to stay. The argument over it had in fact reached a danger point that made staying necessary, even though one sensed a certain hysteria in the insistence. And my latter hours are filled with a perplexed wondering as to how I may leave a fragrant memory. Were I Hercules I would descend into hell and bring back at least the missing squab.

At the other extreme is the barbarian host, stretching me out to make me fit his bed. For I must be taken to view the new real estate extension, and inspect the reconstructed town hall. Whether I am weary or not, there must be a party; I must, at regular intervals, move to a more comfortable chair; and a reluctant Bobbie must be summoned from his play so that I may hear him say his piece.

Well do I recall a committee of ladies appointed to receive the visiting lecturer. "We have nothing to do all the morning," they assured him gayly, "but to make your stay a pleasant one. What would you most enjoy doing?"

Words trembled on his tongue but were not allowed to become vocal. "First, my husband's office," said one; "and I know he would love to show you over the factory. While he is doing that we can attend to a few little things."

"Then a drive out the new boulevard," said another. "My car can pick him up at the factory without the least inconvenience. Henry won't be wanting it until afternoon."

But a third was not to be gainsaid. "He must see the

civic museum. I am tremendously interested in it," she
explained. "There aren't any other cities of this size
that have one. Old maps," she waved an indicative
hand; "early deeds, daguerreotypes, and some of the
most interesting portraits of leading citizens; old fur-
niture"—she waved both hands,—"and shingles from
the first house, and—and—that sort of thing," she
ended vaguely.

"But he hasn't said what he'd most like to do," broke
in the first. "What would you most like to do?" she
asked him archly.

"I wonder," he suggested feebly, "if I might wash?
And then do you suppose I might just sort of lie around
somewhere and not bother you?"

There was an outburst of delighted laughter. "Of
course you can wash! There is a place at the factory
office. But you're not bothering us a bit, and we couldn't
be so inhospitable as to leave you by yourself. Why,
we couldn't have you going away without seeing our
city."

Greek hospitality is the nobler of the two extremes;
but it is likely to be too noble. Few guests, when well
settled into the bosom of the home, can remain long
unaware of sacrifices; which means that sooner or later
they are ill at ease, with nothing to be done about it.
The worst hospitality of our best households is likely

to be Greek; but our community and national hospitality is nearly always procrustean.

Just after the war, when the allies were exchanging compliments instead of duns and I.O.U.'s, Uncle Sam was host to many a distinguished visitor, from grizzled warriors to prime ministers and potentates. In whispers I have been told of the visit of a well-loved king and his gracious lady to our shores. States and cities were clamorous in their demands that he should be routed in their direction. Local politicians brought pressure to bear upon the State Department. Mayors and governors felt that to secure a local appearance of a reigning king and queen would affect the voters more favorably than would even the winning of several government appropriations. So it was planned that His Majesty should be stretched to fit our bed. The royal tour was to last for twenty days, and nineteen nights were to be spent on a sleeper! There was no Theseus to save him, but the king saved himself. Knowing something of America, he insisted upon seeing his itinerary, and then politely asked that it be changed.

But sturdy old Marshal Foch could not protect himself so effectively. His journey across the continent gave city after city an opportunity to add to his weariness by showing itself off. When he would have a little quiet he must review a parade three hours long; when he would sleep he must eat his way through another banquet. No city or town asked what he would most enjoy; but all seized the opportunity to add to his exhaustion. A caption in a Chicago paper lingers in my memory: "Though Enjoying His Trip, Foch Asks It Be Eased Up a Bit." God forgive us for the chicken we fed him; not because he preferred chicken, but because we wished to prove the skill of our French chefs. As he was leaving our shores he remarked that he could never look another hen in the face.

General Fayolle made a three weeks' visit, representing the French army. I glean these extracts from a Parisian interview with him upon his return home. "It has been a hard fight, those three weeks in America. I come back on the verge of collapse, with grim dyspepsia holding me in its grip. . . . There were many banquets and luncheons. I survived them all. . . . I lived through it," concluded the General, *"but even the organizers of my tour had to admit that it was a record for endurance."*

I recall a dinner arranged by an association of artists to honor Mark Twain. The back cover of the menu was left blank except for the information provided in brutal type that the space was for autographs. Before the honored guest had begun his final course, a procession formed and filed slowly past his chair. For three-quarters of an hour with hardly a break he shook hands and produced autographs, until he was physically weary and his good humor destroyed.

If a single host is so often tempted to imitate Procrustes, what is one to expect from a whole host of hosts? Charles Dickens suffered a heavy drain on his health during his tour of America, and was frequently ill. Autograph fiends, clubs, committees and self-important people left him no privacy or time for rest, and too little was done to protect him, by any truly hospitable person with authority. He was lopped off to fit our bed; and from Dickens to the latest Prince of Wales such episodes have constantly repeated themselves.

The Greeks chose their word for it with a certain satiric humor. *Euxenos* meant "hospitality" rightly enough, but etymologically it meant the friendliness of the Black Sea. Now any one who is a guest of the Black Sea can on occasion have a very rough time of it. The Greeks were hospitable in order to please the gods. Their code required that the host should make every necessary and possible sacrifice, and if the guest didn't in his secret heart enjoy it, that was nobody's fault but his. If the lobster Newburg gave him ptomaine poisoning, the benignant gods would still gaze down approvingly upon that hostess who had sacrificed time and strength to prepare the stuff. Lo, she had done it for the sake of a guest, when she knew that crackers and milk would have better suited her own family's taste, digestion, and pocketbook. The fact that her household also suffered went to prove there was no discrimination. So she could be blessed by a sense of duty well done and sing softly to herself as she changed the sheets in the guestroom. If her late guest somewhere out in the world was not enjoying his ptomaine let him reflect that he might better have stayed at home in the first place and eaten his own crackers and milk.

The Procrustean theory of hospitality is that the host shall not bother so much about the gods, but please himself. Nowadays there are few who possess the simple primitive frankness of the founder of that cult. We modern procrusteans are forever denying our real objective, even to ourselves. If we compel a guest to sit in a drizzle watching three miles of parade, we tell ourselves that he must want to see it. If we force him to drink some home-made concoction which we have stirred with an overweening and unjustifiable pride, it is because we keep telling ourselves that he must be thirsty.

Think of the thousands of guests who have broken their teeth upon beaten biscuit in southern homes, or have eaten scrapple in Philadelphia, or snails in San

Francisco, under the eager and compelling gaze of the lady of the house, while their stomachs writhed in revolt.

At this very moment of writing ten thousand persons singled out for attention in as many homes or villages or cities are being immolated upon the altar of local or family pride; and with fixed smiles upon their faces, are hearing Susie recite, or watching the local fire company squirt, or enduring a speech by the representative of the mayor.

Hospitality is derived primarily from the word *hospis* meaning a host, generally one who received pay for the care of guests. *Hospitalita* meant what they got in return for their money. There is a legend somewhere (or if there isn't there ought to be) of a certain innkeeper whose door stood open to the high road between Baluchistan and Bagdad. Now the fame of this inn or hospital had spread from the Iberian peninsula to the furthest confines of Cathay by reason of its cookery. Its recipes had been handed down from father to son for many generations,—a jovial succession of rubicund cooks who enjoyed their own cooking. For always mine host himself directed the mixtures of the soups and stews and compotes. Travelers who had sojourned there in the dark ages left dying wishes that their sons should some day be guests at that inn; so the family tradition of being a guest there was as firmly established as the tradition of landlordship. Then at last came tragedy; for an only son inherited the estate who could not learn to cook. That heaven-sent attribute simply was not in him. Yet he was forever trying and, as years came upon him, forever more desperate. Travelers passed that way from all corners of the earth, but after one meal were prone to hurry on; until at length he made it a rule that no guests might stop unless they tarried for a week. In such an interval he felt that they might be trained to like his cooking. The only result of this device, however, was that at the end of the week they could not leave, so that in time the inn grew into a vast caravansary, with a great proportion of its rooms devoted to the care of the sick. Thus it was that the word *hospital* acquired its modern meaning.

So we perceive that the human notion of hospitality has undergone many vicissitudes. Some men have been hospitable to please the gods, and others—the great majority—to please themselves. It remains for a race to appear upon this footstool who are instinctively hospitable in order to please their guests. This we may call the utopian brand.

XVII

Self-Esteem

HOSPITALITY, either as a manner or a moral, descends from the notion that one ought to consider the happiness of his neighbor before his own. But there is a bothersome thought that occurs to me in connection with that command to love thy neighbor as thyself. If you do not love yourself very much, then you need not love your neighbor any more than that. If you hold yourself in contempt, you are permitted to be contemptuous of all your neighbors. Conversely, it looks as though the whole moral structure rests upon a decent amount of self-respect, even self-esteem.

If morals and manners grow out of self-respect, I am troubled about the one-talent man. I have always had a sneaking sympathy for that fellow in the Bible who buried his talent. "I was afraid" he said, "and so I buried it in the earth." Then the master took it away from him and gave it to some one who already had a lot of other talents. So the poor fellow must have lost his self-respect, and then his morals, and finally his manners.

The pitiful thing is that the man with one talent should so often be afraid. People like Leonardo, who could do almost anything and do it well, seem to have no particular shyness about trying their hands at painting or architecture or inventing machinery. But George W. Jones, with one little talent—perhaps it is a fairly good voice, perhaps it is some knack with his hands, perhaps it is only an aptitude for recognizing the beauty in homely things—feels that his gift is so small and lonesome that he cannot be positive it is a talent at all.

The scriptural story says that he was afraid of his master "for he knew that he was a hard man." But nine times out of ten I think that what he fears most is laughter. These five-talent people often have enough assurance or egotism to protect them from a whole cyclone of laughter. They are sure that it is meant for somebody else, or that it is a cyclone of applause. But that humble-minded one-talent man hears a laugh; it shatters with its vibrations the little protecting shelter that he has shyly erected to cover his tests of that talent's worth. So he buries the talent, and it rusts away. And the greatest tragedy about it all is that oftentimes the destroying laughter which he hears is his own.

The law of life seems just a bit cruel in its treatment of that man. And I am sure I could like him better than the one with five talents, if only he were not afraid.

XVIII

Whittling

THERE is this to be said for a good hobby,—it helps
one to preserve whatever modicum of common sense
he already possesses, and sets up a current of sympathy
between many wide-flung children of that amateur
gardener, Adam.

This social aspect is important. For one who is not
by instinct a joiner, there is much to be said for my idea
of joining the human race; and the devotee of a hobby
finds himself united by pleasant bonds with a surprising number of his fellow amateurs, without such
encumbrances as presidents, and executive secretaries,
and dues, and minutes of the preceding meetings.

Consider stamp collectors, for instance. They throng
to the stamp auctions from Paris to San Francisco, yet
there are no by-laws that require their attendance, and
no roll calls. They exchange greetings as though they
were fellow-members of something-or-other, bound
together by the ties of a common interest.

The hobbyist must be always an amateur in the true sense of the word. He may sell something he has made or collected, so long as that was not his object in making or collecting; but if he keeps on selling the products of his hobby, then obviously he has gone into that business.

Any interest becomes a hobby only when it is wholly unrelated to the vocation from which one earns a living. A crockery manufacturer who collects old china does not qualify. He is quite properly making himself more of a crockery expert.

Any sincerely cultivated hobby demands a lot of earnest research. True hobbyists, knowing that, gain respect for one another, which is a good thing. I have a near and dear relative who affects early glass. This involves acquaintance with out-of-the-way places, and a technical knowledge of manufacturing methods in various decades, and familiarity with water-marks, or whatever they call them, and manufacturers' names,— all of which compel my grudging respect, even though I myself cannot distinguish a piece of Sandwich glass from late Woolworth or early Kresge.

But collectors make up only a small percentage of the entire brotherhood. There are the artificers, medical men who have tool benches in the cellar, insurance men who etch, lawyers who sneak into the kitchen, when the maid is out, and cook. As for me, I whittle.

A whittler may have the satisfying sense of belonging to an ancient and honorable brotherhood; and like all true hobbyists he recognizes another of his tribe almost instinctively. For the sincere whittler cannot pass by an odd bit of wood, or a stick beside the path, without glancing at it appraisingly, while his right hand twitches toward the trouser pocket where he keeps his jack-knife. With blade and stick in contact he sits on the edges of things and proceeds to scatter shavings. If he can spit with accuracy, so much the better. I do not know why this is a characteristic, but so it seems to be. I cannot spit skillfully enough as yet to merit the thirty-third degree in whittling, but when a certain one of my remaining front teeth comes out, I hope to arrive.

My apprenticeship as a whittler was served as a boy in New England and in a day when men really whittled; and I began, of course, with a willow whistle. Just how or when I happened to make the first one I have no idea. One could not be a small boy without a knife, or have a knife and not know how to make a whistle. I do remember, though, that an old man taught me to put a dried pea inside so that the whistle would trill; and I know that I myself learned to cut two holes in the bark to produce two notes, and made the home miserable for the balance of the willow season. That old man is a sainted memory. He made boats in bottles, and houses with figures inside too large to fit through the doors or windows. He had always whittled as long as men could remember. It was said of him, and generally believed, that when he was born he whittled his way out and at once carved his initials on his own cradle. With such saints still living, no wonder boys whittled in the golden age.

After a willow whistle, the next steps, as every one knows, are the little utilitarian things, such as slingshots, bows and arrows, boats, wooden daggers and other weapons of war. There was a small gun, I remember, simple to make but realistic in appearance, which mounted a rubber band held taut by a trigger, and shot small squares of pasteboard surprising distances in a schoolroom. When I have laid this writing aside I think that I shall make another, after these many years.

While these simple necessities were developing a true technique, artistic impulses were struggling for utterance. A lady's fan was generally its first expression. We made them for our mothers or sisters, or—shyly—for extraneous little girls. They were lacy, dainty little things that looked much more difficult than they really were. An oblong stick of straight-grained pine was the basis, and the only difficult work was an even slicing of the leaves, after the edges had been carved to suit the fancy; then the wood was soaked and the leaves spread out and dried. I should like to show you one. But the whittler had arrived at maturity when he could make a wooden chain of several unbroken links, ending in a little cage containing a ball that rolled around inside, but could not escape between the bars.

Such was the proper training of a young whittler. Its place in the scheme of things was taken for granted, and it yielded in due course to other juvenile arts and crafts. Only when it was carried on into later life and developed and applied, did it become a hobby.

Looking back over many years of such industry in idleness, I can plead that whittling makes for friendships in odd places, and enjoyment of outdoors for one who is not an athlete, and such cleansing of the mind, when it is cluttered up, as any good hobby should provide.

Walking sticks held my interest over a long period. One learns the qualities of different woods, and to recognize many varieties of tree with such qualities in mind. The true whittler is not destructive. He takes a branch only when the lopping of it will add to a tree's symmetry or strength; and a sapling only when it grows too close to a neighbor. It was the search for outgrowing roots to form grotesque figures atop my canes that led me all unsuspectingly toward modernism and a new school of whittling.

Already there are a number of disciples. Until a better name evolves, we are Doodoo-ists, and our motto is "Nature starts it and we finish it." We walk abroad looking for such odd growths of root or branch as suggest men and animals. The knife merely completes what nature evidently intended to do in the first place, but then changed her mind and did the commonplace thing. It is a canon of this art that glue should not be used, or other artificial jointing. If the figures possess legs and arms they must grow there; accomplishing the purpose in any other way is cheating. I have, for instance, a graceful long-legged crane brought to me by a friend from Hawaii, the work of native Japanese. I am told that they are selling many such things to tourists. It is a twisted root, rich in natural color, and pleasing to the eye. You may imagine my shock of disillusionment when I discovered that one leg had no natural connection with the parent root, but had been skillfully attached. How can I trust the Japanese after that?

Some day I shall write a book about the adventures of a whittler. But life grows richer as I grow older, and the longer I put it off the better the book will be. On the whole, I think I had better make it a posthumous volume. New England has perhaps been the richest field for experience. More than once I have sat down beside a taciturn old inhabitant of my native section and whittled him into garrulity. If I could spit better it might have taken a shorter time.

"Hank allers looked so wise, seemed 's if we oughter use him some place where folks didn't know him so well; so we sent him to congress. Now he's lookin' wiser every year. Great big cloud without any rain."

"I see Widder Tuttle's oldest boy yesterday; the fat one. He was hurryin' down Center Street hill. Too damn lazy to hold back."

Such are the gems of conversation that my memory associates with whittling bees. I have glimpsed the proprietor of a wayside garage whittling in front of his shop, and have known instantly that I should stop there to have the internal organs of my car examined. I know a schoolmaster in Massachusetts whose wise counsels have started a host of boys upon worthy careers. He walks out with them individually, and when you see his glance questing here and there along the path, and his hand reaching into a trouser pocket for his knife, you know that the conference is going to be richly productive.

Somewhere along the New England coast I happened into a ship-model shop. The room was full of little boats, fascinating in their miniature perfection. All types and designs, literally from all parts of the world, were sent there to be repaired or re-rigged, some of them valued at fabulous amounts. Almost the first thing that caught my attention was the simplicity of the shop's equipment and the absence of elaborate tools. I mentioned this to the proprietor, who seemed pleased at the comment. "Everything I do in this place," he said, "could be done with no more equipment than a good pocket knife, and glue and string. The tools I use just save time; they don't do the work any better."

Yet there is nothing in New England's atmosphere to develop whittling, and I do not believe that the art is indigenous there. In Brionde, a small village in central France, tourists crowd about a wooden clock which was made by a native craftsman in 1640 with no tools other than a small knife. It has kept good time for three hundred years. A few years ago when my wife and I were idling among New England lakes in our car, we came upon a boys' camp whose director proved to be an old friend. He persuaded us to stop over for a few days and I was to pay for the sojourn by giving his boys some instruction in whittling. An alarming number seemed eager for the experience, but only three or four had pocket knives. I had always supposed that a boy without a knife was an incomplete boy. We bought out a village store and then started for a willow patch. I shall never do it again without a trained nurse in attendance. Before the first successful whistle had squeaked those youngsters were squirting blood in all directions. They whittled their own thumbs and they whittled one another; yet they ranged in age from twelve to sixteen years. New England is going to perdition.

The whittler finds no geographic limitations. The manzanita bush in the southwest twists into alluringly contorted dancers and fabulous beasts and Laocoön groups. When fresh cut it is carved easily, and then hardens to iron, while its rich terracotta-colored bark sets permanently in place. The core of the cholla cactus, branching in effective ways, is a marvel of nature's engineering skill. Constructed like lattice work it is light and delicate in appearance, but however slender has surprising rigidity and tensile strength. Canes made from it, and handles for salad forks or hearth brushes or umbrellas are dainty and out of the ordinary. I have a little stool made from cholla which looks as flimsy as any *objet d'art,* but for a dozen years has borne the weight of visitors at our fireside. At first I looked for half-dead stalks whose thorny covering had dried and peeled away from the core. But with a long knife and gloved hands one may strip the skin from a fresh stem as it grows, and then cut off what is needed. There need be no trouble of conscience over destructiveness, for broken sections falling to the ground will take root where they fall and grow quickly to be the bane of cattle or pedestrians. An Indian trader told me of another method. Cut the stem that is desired, pour sweetened water on it and push it to an ant hill, and the ants will clean it to its fair white skeleton.

But a whittler on the desert may find himself in paradise, with bones scattered about. What the ants might do for a cactus stem, the coyotes have done to the bones. Here one needs instead of the pocket knife a couple of slender files and a hack-saw blade. The clean white vertebrae of sheep or cows, or of smaller wild animals, have natural forms that call for little imagination. Every tourist knows the heads of horned cattle that cowboys wear, like old-fashioned necktie rings, to hold kerchief ends together. With these to suggest the way, one may devise odd little four-legged beasts, and priests with flapping robes, and bats with spread wings.

I owe a pleasant experience to one of these carvings. We were spending some weeks with an Indian trader, in the mountains of the Navajo Reservation on the border between New Mexico and Arizona. All of one morning a silent Indian had been sitting on the counter in the trader's store, meditating on what he should purchase. I had passed him a dozen times as I went in and out, and had greeted him each time. But there was no word in reply, no change of expression on his poker face. My English apparently meant nothing to him, and my companionship was not desired. Outside the store I had been contriving a sort of miniature totem pole from four or five vertebrae one on the other. A little paint in gay colors made a picturesque object of it and I carried it into the office, to show the trader what a strange antiquity I had uncovered. As I passed that stoic Indian, he glanced at the thing in my hand, slid from his high seat and reached for it silently. I passed it over, and he turned it about, eyeing it gravely. Then he handed it back. "Very interesting," he remarked. "Looks a good deal like Japanese art." One may whittle even the woodenest of Indians into speech.

But speaking of bones, my conscience is disturbed for the first time in a long career as a whittler; and the cause is in the Indian country. As increasing numbers of tourists are discovering our southwest, there is an increasing demand for souvenirs of all sorts; trinkets and gewgaws, in addition to the fine products of Indian craftsmanship in silver work and weaving. As the demand grows there are always white men eager to profit by it. The tourist is protected by law as well as commercial good sense, and only goods actually made by Indians can be so labeled. However it is quite possible for an enterprising merchant to employ an Indian in his shop and set him to work on the embellishment of factory products. Here is Indian craftsmanship in letter if not in spirit; and as a result the gift shops are flooded with things that Indians never would have dreamed of making,—wrist watch bracelets, baby spoons, napkin rings, ladies' purses. Now and then the white man goes a little further, or even the whole distance, and turns out Indian gifts himself. Katchina dolls, those little figures decorated with paint and feathers, representing Indian household gods, are now being turned out in quantity by non-Indian artizans.

During an early visit to the Navajo Reservation, I left a little trail of carved bones with friends and acquaintances. The simplest form was a bat with spread wings carved from the vertebra of a cow and needing little hand-work to make an amusing grotesque. Last summer along the highway through the Painted Desert I saw these same little creatures on shelves in several of the tourist shops. They looked startlingly familiar and eyed me reproachfully. There was no question about it! I was at least the grand-parent of a large number of Indian curios, and it would be necessary only for the white man who was making them to employ a few

Indians in his shop and they would become Indian-
made goods. Twenty years from now some wise young
Columbia graduate-student who is writing a Ph.D.
thesis on primitive arts or craftsmanship will discover
that particular bat-form to be Mongolian, handed down
from the days of Kubla Khan. Then a piece of one of
them may be found in a cliff dwelling; for I know that
I sat in one of those homes of a long-dead race and
carved at such a bone while my wife prepared lunch
near the ancient hearth-stone. If I abandoned some
unfinished bit of craftsmanship in that spot, the legend
will be irretrievably established. If I try to prove that
I invented it, I shall be laughed out of court by a
hundred museum directors, and a thousand graduate-
students, and half a million purveyors of souvenirs.

They say that as a man grows older his thoughts
revert more frequently to childhood. My first boyish
enthusiasm for whittling was aroused by the sight of a
ship in a bottle; and now I am making them, and at
last realizing a small boy's ambition. I began with a
two-masted schooner in a milk bottle, and gradually
reduced the neck of the bottle and increased the size
of the ship.

There are many things to learn about the business,
by a process of trial and error. On one occasion I got
an intricate boat all set up inside the glass and became

ambitious to see some realistic waves about it; so I poured in liquid plaster of Paris tinted to the proper shade of green. I did not realize that this material when it sets must supersaturate the air about it. Every mast and spar had been stepped in glue and the rigging had been attached in the same way, and before my eyes the entire ship disintegrated. Now I use enamel paint of the right tint and all goes well. From that first milk bottle I have at last progressed to a full-rigged ship in a whisky flask; which may be the *summa cum* of the art, since the flask must be emptied first.

But my old heart is breaking. I have seen in a *Gifte Shoppe* a "knock-down" ship, factory made, already to set up inside an accompanying bottle. I am glad that I am not part of such a world as that; and I grow eager for the happy insensitiveness of second childhood, when I shall go about again carving my initials on trees.

XIX

—isms in Art

In the days of the Boer War, an artist friend of mine went to South Africa to make battle-field sketches for a famous illustrated paper. That conflict saw the first use of smokeless powder; and it was the first real war in which British troops deployed and dug themselves in. Until then British soldiers had dressed themselves up in clothes that would make the best possible target and marched forward in serried ranks that no enemy gunner could miss. But in South Africa they broke ranks and fought from any shelter they could devise.

My friend made his sketches and watched with youthful eagerness for their appearance on the printed page. To his horror he found that some one back in the art editor's office had added battle smoke to his sketches, and had put uniforms on soldiers who were in reality stripped to the waist and covered with mud.

Naturally, when he got back he voiced his protest. But the editor was unashamed.

"You want to convey the truth," he said; "you paint a battle scene, and want your public to know that death is in the air. Powder smoke is the hieroglyphic which denotes a death-dealing rifle ball. Until our public has learned some other symbol, we have to use that one.

"You see pictures in the comic papers of two men talking together; there are little balloons coming out of their mouths, containing printed words. You do not think those balloons are really there; that is merely the device by which the artist succeeds in telling you that the words are being spoken. As you grow more intelligent you do not need the balloons. The spoken words can be printed below the picture, and you will know that they are being spoken.

"It is the same way with those uniforms. Our readers are not yet able to believe that a battle is in progress unless they see men facing one another wearing different tunics. We had to paint something in, to indicate British against Boer, and we shall have to continue doing so until our audience understands new symbols. So you see we have tried to make your sketches convey more truth, not less, to our readers."

The techniques of the various arts are the symbols by which artists communicate their emotional experiences. Perhaps a time comes when an audience outgrows the need for some particular device. Certainly artists themselves often grow weary of one sign language, or feel that it fails to perform its task, and then they find a new one. But they must work without the incentive of appreciation, until an audience assembles which is able to read the new code.

Certainly a man might be the greatest poet in the world and yet, if he wrote in French to an audience that understood only English, never be appreciated.

When I see an unintelligible painting, or hear a bit of "discordant" music or read a poem which seems to me to have neither rhythm nor meaning, I wonder if the creator of it is really a great artist who speaks a language I have not yet learned. So many artists nowadays are abandoning the old symbols and hieroglyphics of communication that I feel woefully ignorant. I do not want to laugh at a Netherlander because his Dutch speech sounds like gibberish to me. Perhaps he has something interesting to say, and I would gain great profit if I could understand him. I do not want to be among those who laugh at new techniques in painting or music or literature because they seem so odd. I should like first of all to learn the new language, if I possibly can, in order to understand.

I thought I had gotten a little forwarder in music, unmusical as I am, when I overheard this conversation between a radical composer and a critic:

"You call that composition of yours the 'Embankment March,' " said his questioner, "yet it is not in 2-4 or 6-8 time. Nobody could march to it."

"I do not want any one to march to it," he said indignantly, "I do not ever want any one to march! That is the way I felt when I saw men marching."

In terms of another art, "although I call this painting 'Nude Descending a Staircase' I am not trying to reproduce such a phenomenon photographically; I am just trying to find a way of telling you how I felt when I saw it happen."

But the trouble is that this is breaking down all of my own personal tests and standards of excellence. Also it is denying me the joy of full response to emotional appeals through art. It is very easy for the trickster and the incompetent to insist that they are saying something important when they are not; and it takes me such a long time to learn French, when I don't know any, or Naturalism or Stream-of-Consciousness-ism when I am acquainted with only the old hieroglyphics. But I want to be sure that I do not laugh too soon.

XX

Recognizing a Philosopher When You See One

IT SEEMS strange that during the ninety years since his first book appeared, Edward Lear has been generally regarded as a humorist, even as a writer of nonsense. Yet not so strange; for he was an Englishman. Those of his fellow-countrymen who first glimpsed his writings were doubtless perplexed. It is in fact a matter of record that the first British critic who happened upon his book ejaculated "Haw." A second one also said "Haw." A third, hearing the two ejaculations closely following one another and thinking that they emanated from the same man, assumed that the book was funny. This rumor spread until it became a national obsession; and as a result the profound philosophical emanations of Edward Lear, compact and concise beyond parallel, concealing their epigrammatic crypticism under a mantle of apparent simplicity, were very nearly lost to the world.

Great philosophers, like great poets, have invariably possessed prophetic vision. Lear was no exception. I should like to touch upon only two or three of his theses which deal richly with present-day problems.

His views upon education were writ large for those who care to read. Faddism depressed him: "There was an old man with a beard," he writes, thus aptly characterizing our school system as an off-shoot, "who said it is just as I feared; two owls and a hen, four larks and a wren, have all made their nests in my beard." With gentle sarcasm he points to the "old man of Dumbree who taught little owls to drink tea; for he said 'to eat mice is not proper or nice'; that amiable man of Dumbree!" He points also, in parable, to the "old lady of France who taught little ducklings to dance," and he offers advice to inadequate teachers of these futile subjects when he adds, "There was an old man of Dundalk, who tried to teach fishes to walk. When they tumbled down dead he grew weary and said, 'I had better go back to Dundalk.'"

Yet in all of Lear's philosophy he is never the obstinate conservative. With startling directness he does away with Greek, rather than continue it in our modern one-legged fashion: "There was an old person of Cromer, who stood on one leg to read Homer; when he found he grew stiff he jumped over the cliff, which concluded that person of Cromer."

The multiplicity of textbooks written by incompetents receives his attention: "There was a young person whose history was always considered a mystery; she sat in a ditch, although no one knew which, [note this picture of a historian without horizons] and composed a small treatise on history."

Our efforts to pour knowledge into the young at our educational filling stations meet with his disapproval: "There was an old man at a station, who made a promiscuous oration; but they said 'take some snuff!— you have talked quite enough, you afflicting old man at a station.'"

So cogent are Lear's views upon preparedness versus a doctrine of passive resistance, that one might believe he foresaw today's perplexities. Observe the state of China, he says; a land of wise philosophers who nevertheless have been blind to danger: "There was an old man of Hong Kong who never did anything wrong [sublime sarcasm]. He lay on his back with his head in a sack, that innocuous old man of Hong Kong." Then he continues in the same vein to cite the incident of the man "who supposed that the street door was partially closed; but some very large rats ate his coats and his hats [obviously referring to the treaty ports and Manchuria] while that futile old gentleman dozed." Then he defines non-resistance in terms of the "man who said how shall I flee from this horrible cow? I will sit on this stile and continue to smile, which may soften the heart of that cow."

Lear's own acceptance of the theory of armament for defense, and even aggression, is so often indicated in terms of women that he evidently foresaw not only a state of universal female suffrage, but a world governed by militant femininity. There was "the young lady of Hull who was chased by a virulent bull; but she seized on a spade and called out "Who's afraid?' " Also the treatment which the young lady from Troy accorded her annoyers: "Some she killed with a thump, some she drowned at the pump, and some she took with her to Troy"—captives of her bow and spear. The militant male is in fact surprisingly absent from Lear's cosmos. But he seems to have foreseen at least one of our international gestures toward peace in the midst of a militaristic world, and to have had his doubts as to its practicality; for he wrote, "There was an old man at the Hague whose ideas were excessively vague; he built a balloon to examine the moon, that deluded old man of the Hague."

Lear's prophetic vision is best proved in his treatment of that eternal controversy between radical and con-

servative. Who can deny that he foresaw the great
Slavic experiment: "There was a young lady of Russia
who screamed so that no one could hush her. Her
screams were extreme—no one heard such a scream as
was screamed by that lady of Russia." On the other
hand he seems to have small sympathy for the tradi-
tionalism that causes another of his symbolic old men
to "run up and down in his grandmother's gown."
Between these two extremes he visions America, "Man
of the West, who never could get any rest," vacillating
from one extreme to the other,—"so they set him to
spin on his nose and his chin, which cured that old man
of the West."

He even glimpses us in the throes of our present
social discussion. There is the young "parlor radical"
who advocates political overturn without knowing what
she is talking about: "There was a young person in
pink who called out for something to drink; but they
said, O my daughter, there's nothing but water, which
vexed that young person in pink."

The timid citizen who lives in constant fear of communists is suggested by "the person in black,—a grass-
hopper jumped on his back; when it chirped in his ear
he was smitten with fear," while the witch-hunting
type of journalist and legislator is satirized in "There
was an old man who said 'Hush! I perceive a young

bird in this bush!' When they said, 'Is it small?' he replied, 'Not at all; It is four times as big as the bush!' "

Lear seems, on the whole, to be a hopeful prophet so far as we are concerned; though there are those who insist that his great narrative poem "The Jumblies" is a masterly and prophetic satire upon America under the present Administration: "They went to sea in a sieve, they did; in a sieve they went to sea."

Throughout all of Lear's writings we discern the philosophic commentator smiling benignly upon human weaknesses and foibles; from the food faddist "who dined on one pea and one bean; for he said 'More than that would make me too fat,' "—to the pseudo-literary poetess and mystic "whose ways were perplexing and odd; she purchased a whistle, and sat on a thistle and squeaked to the people of Jodd."

If there is ever any harshness in his commentary upon human failings it is toward intolerance, as when he describes the martyrdom of the "old man of Thermopylae who never did anything properly" and exposes the conformist neighbors "who said if you choose to boil eggs in your shoes you shall never remain in Thermopylae." He is even more bitter against those who establish immigration quotas, displaying a distrust of foreigners merely because they are untidy, as in the case of the "old person of Bow whom nobody happened to know [what a diatribe against snobbishness!] so they gave him some soap and said coldly we hope you will go back directly to Bow."

Tolerant and liberal as Lear evidently is, yet we find him urging the comfortable doctrine of social conformity. Nowhere is this more clearly enunciated than in his great poem, only a few lines of which we here quote:

There lived an old man in the Kingdom of Tess
Who invented a purely original dress;
And when it was perfectly made and complete
He opened the door and walked into the street.
[Here follow several stanzas realistically descriptive of social persecution; then—]

He tried to run back to his house, but in vain,
For scores of fat pigs came again and again;
They rushed out of stables and hovels and doors;
They tore off his stockings, his shoes and his drawers;

They swallowed the last of his shirt with a squall
Whereon he ran home with no clothes on at all.

And he said to himself as he bolted the door
"I will not wear a similar dress any more,
Any more, any more, any more, never more!"

Thus we leave Lear, trusting that this humble bit of research may arouse in others an ambition to know better that great philosopher (branded as humorist for four generations) whom Tennyson and Ruskin delighted to honor,—and surely neither one of them would have recognized a humorist when he saw one.

XXI

Perhaps I Too Am Musical

THERE is this to be said for some of the more radical forms of music, painting, and sculpture,—they give us the comfortable feeling that we, too, might be able to do something of the sort. In the old days any pleasure that I gained from strolling through a picture gallery, or sitting through an orchestral concert was always tempered by a sense of my own futility. For even to me often came those creative moments when I longed to splash a sunset upon canvas, or else burst into song; and I dared not.

But a new day has brought heart's ease. Since I have come to know the work of certain modern painters I say to myself, "Why should I not paint, if I happen to feel like it?" And I have listened to some modern symphonic music that has sent me home triumphantly asserting, "I shall sing if I want to; anywhere, any time. What is a dissonance but some perfect expression of an inward state; what is a flatted note but a protest? To be off-key is not only a right but a privilege!"

By way of celebrating this spiritual release I have already painted several pictures, and am in the process of composing a symphony or two. May I outline one of the latter? The idea for it came to me as I was driving home from a concert the other evening. Suddenly I realized that the raucous noises of traffic and all of the harsh city night sounds assumed new significance. Following my simple custom I stopped at a corner drugstore and sat on a high stool at its soda counter: and as I listened to the assorted noises of the place this theme developed.

THE CORNER DRUGSTORE

A Symphonic Tone-Poem

1st Movement (*a capriccio*)

The percussion instruments are dominant, and suggest the clatter of glasses on the soda counter, the shifting of chairs around little tables, scraping of feet; then (*poco a poco*) the fainter sounds of the compounding of prescriptions with a pestle. Muted violins and one French horn in a *cadenza* suggest book-worms arguing in front of the loan-library shelves. *Agitato ad fine* implies that most of the books are mystery stories.

2nd Movement (*allegro non troppo*)

The human element in the poem assumes dominance. Shrill chatter of young voices. Young men purchasing sodas for young women (bassoons and saxophones *glasé a frappé caramello*). Wise cracks from the soda clerk explain a shrill theme from the flute (*coco a colo*). Another theme which reappears throughout this movement (*calando*), diminishing steadily in power, is the sucking sound of straws in emptying soda glasses. This is skillfully done by the reversal of the flutes and clarinets, the musicians all rising and blowing through the wrong ends. The movement accelerates (*carbono efferveso*). Professors from a neighboring college enter the shop; extreme discords denote a botanist arguing with two psychologists, both suddenly harmonizing to unite in an attack upon a philosopher. All of this is carried by the woodwinds. The movement ends with the introduction of a new theme that will lead imperceptibly into the final movement,—the plaintive cry of a mendicant selling pencils. This is a sustained minor from the hobo.

3rd Movement (*Medulla oblongato in a flat*)

This opens with a reminder that the drugstore has an important function other than social. Violas, 'cellos, and bass vials [sic] denote the moans of the sick (*ammonia spirito*). Throughout this movement an ever recurrent note from the tuba (*con prescriptioné*) suggests the entrance of a fat man seeking relief from persistent hiccoughs. The first movement is recalled again by the percussions,—and then we are suddenly reminded that the soda clerk is making a banana split (bassoon, trombone and traps, *chocolado con vanillo*). This food theme is subtly carried further by the pickelo and bones. The climax of the entire symphony, with its rare blending of idealism and practicality (*rubarbo con sodio*), is approached by the brasses, suggesting the honking motor horns of impatient swains anxious to get away after spending money; the clatter of washing glasses; and the scraping of sidewalk signs being brought in for the night. A grand final crash indicates that the composer and his wife have said good night to their friends, gotten into their car, and a back tire has blown out.

The outline set down here is merely suggestive. It is of course to be written in atonic form. If I am able to do more with it I shall dedicate it to my old friends Lawrence Gilman, Dick Aldrich and Will Chase, and then if some one will conduct it I promise to take them all into my corner drugstore after the concert and buy **them a tuba-ful of most** effervescent soda water.

XXII

Learning to Be an Audience

LONG after I had first discovered pleasure in a symphony, I still half believed that the frog-tailed figure in black, gesticulating with his back toward me, was merely a musical convention, and the group of real musicians who faced me carried on in spite of him. Then somehow I learned that an orchestra is a single instrument of many tubes and strings, played upon by the conductor; and I turned that thought over in my mind and found it revealing.

Education comes to the open mind, with or without formal teaching. My elementary education progressed a stage forward when I discovered the place of the conductor in the scheme of things and began to recognize the touch of his hand upon that strange keyboard.

The tone of a violin, I am told, depends upon the quality of the wood of which it is made, a certain perfection of design, even the glue that binds it; the tone of a horn depends upon the blend of metals in its composition, as well as the adjustment of part to part. I knew that each of the players who faced me had considered these factors, and had come to know his instrument even in its temperamental adjustments to changes in the weather.

But what of that multiform instrument upon which the conductor plays with his slender baton, touching it now delicately, now fiercely, now here, now there, now sweeping its every key with one mad gesticulation? Behind every string that he cajoles, every tube that he commands there is the intriguing face of a man, and behind every face there must be human emotions. Even that imperturbable person behind the kettledrums must know joy, sorrow, insomnia, love, anger, indigestion. Here are instruments affected by forces far more varied and indefinable than steam-heat or changing weather. The psychic influence upon them of a thousand listeners sitting beyond the footlights must be incalculable. So I took a further step forward when I realized the place of the audience in the orchestral scheme.

It is the testimony of any lecturer that as he stands upon a platform gazing into massed faces, he can have the current of his thought deflected by one man out of a thousand who edges his way out of a seat and tip-toes down the aisle; or by a woman who drops her gloves, and soon has her neighbors engaged in finding them. If this is true of one man who faces an audience with a wide choice of phrases to interpret his ideas, it may be far more so with the sensitive musician who must have an eye to his notes, and again to the waving baton. If a shifting audience, permitting itself odd relaxations, distracts his attention for a moment from these two things his power is weakened. Then multiply that one player by sixty, some of them especially sensitive to distractions of motion and untoward incident occurring before their eyes, and one may realize what an audience can do to an orchestra.

The other day I sat in my accustomed seat, and watched the throng arriving. It was time for the concert to begin, and still they came. The orchestra was assembled, but the conductor, who had adjusted his habits to that of his public, still waited. Finally he entered and bowed to the friendly applause and took his place. But still the late-comers were arriving. Ushers tried to hold them back, but some pushed through resentfully as though saying, "I am a subscriber, and you have no right to stop me." Others slipped through unobtrusively, a little shame-faced, and wandered about like lost souls in the half-darkness trying to remember just where their seats were. Still others brushed blandly by, cheery smiles upon their faces. They are the "gate crashers" who always go where and when they want, trusting to that bland smile and imperturbability to get away with it. Everywhere was rustling and whispering of apology as late-comers crowded themselves past protuding knees to inside seats.

The conductor waited. Any person sitting in a corner of the auditorium might wonder why; because, after all, the noise in that one corner might not be so great. But all the noise from all the corners combines to throw a volume of rustling, and whispering, and stumbling, and clattering over the footlights where sixty musicians are waiting to merge themselves into one sensitive instrument upon which the conductor is to play.

Somewhere back of my seat two ladies, who are doubtless music lovers, but quite obviously old friends, have come together at this concert after some hours, at least, of separation. They are chattering about a special sale of gowns, and their tones are low but penetrating. They are waiting for the conductor to raise his baton, but they are going to exchange experiences up to the very last second. Oddly enough, the conductor is waiting for them and others of their temper. It seems to be a sort of *impasse*. Finally the conductor breaks it by lifting his baton, and the first strains of the symphony drown out final details as to the cut of an evening gown. But I know that will come later. Between the first and second movements of the symphony the conversation will be resumed.

It takes a great deal of education plus native quality to become an orchestra conductor. It takes a great deal of both to earn a place in the orchestra. It may take something of both to be an audience.

If I knew more about it myself I should write a treatise upon this, and include all of the fine technical points. I know, for instance, that those audiences which are most highly educated musically do not applaud between the movements of a symphony. They do not use that brief space for the exchange of confidences about the cut of a dress. They use it just as the conductor and the orchestra use it,—for relaxation, and readjustment in the chair, for reflection and summarizing, then settling themselves to hear the next movement. It is only at the end of the symphony when the conductor turns, that applause is in order. My friends in the seats behind me are generous with applause, and I am sure that they mean it. But since they are making a noise with the palms of their hands, why should they not with their lips? Conversation begins with them the moment applause begins; multiplied by hundreds of others in every part of the house, what a subdued roar of conversation must be belching over the footlights into the ears of musicians adjusting themselves for the next unit in a symphonic whole!

For lack of musical education I cannot list all of the technical characteristics of a perfect audience. But "though I may not know art, I know what I do not like." I do not like the lady who beats time on the arm of her seat. I do not like the soulful-eyed young man who attitudinizes during the finest moments, so ostentatiously that he forces my attention to waver. I do not like the elderly person who lets various articles of personal property slip off her lap, gropes for them at once, picks them up, and puts them back where they will slip off again. I do not like the man who sneezes into the back of my neck. I do not like the very young lady who emits audible sighs and little breathless adjectives along with her applause, gazing soulfully at me for corroboration. I do not like the man who crunches cough-drops with a noise like a horse feeding; I think I should like him better if he coughed. And above all, I do not like the persons who begin to get ready to start to go as soon as they realize that the symphony is nearing its final measures.

This is a sour fashion of considering folk at concerts. On the other hand, I like those people who arrive on time, and seem to have made some effort in advance to discover where their seats are. And I like those who, having come late by reason of some real emergency, accept the dicta of good taste and concert rules, and neither bribe, cajole, nor threaten an usher, but listen quietly where they are until concert rules permit them to be seated. I like those about me who use the moments between symphonic movements for muscular relaxation, and quiet looking around, and a glance at the program if the light permits, evidently assuming that the world of workaday affairs was abandoned emotionally as well as physically when the concert began, and will be reëntered regretfully only when the concert is over. I like those seat-neighbors who, having arrived on time and settled themselves to a complete enjoyment of the concert, insist upon enjoying it thoroughly to the last note, and are not concerned as to whether their hats or galoshes are within reach; nor do they apologize sibilantly because the effort to get themselves into a coat has led to the jabbing of a neighbor in the ribs.

It must be hard to be a conductor. I am told that it is difficult to learn to play a violin, or even a kettledrum. But it is almost as hard for some people to learn to be an audience, and there are those, I suspect, who never will acquire it.

XXIII

Conversation

THE word "conversation," most excellent Theophilus, in its root-meaning implies a discovery of what the other fellow has to say. So it is quite evident that we have been applying the term to a lot of human talk which does not deserve it. Whispering together at the theater or concert while the performance is going on, for instance, comes under that other head of manners and morals.

But words are forever growing beyond their roots; and if I may revise the dictionary I suggest that there are four sorts of conversation generally practiced among human beings; to wit:

(A) Each participant is gaining for himself pleasure or relief by talking.

(B) One participant is trying to convince or instruct the others, who are either actively or passively resisting.

(C) All participants are simultaneously trying to inform or convince one another.

(D) Each participant is trying to discover the ideas of the others on any given subject.

Form A seems to be most generally practiced. One hears it among children at play, and sometimes at what are called "social calls." When a specialist in any field flaunts the vocabulary of his kind while talking to laymen, he is using Form A.

Form B occurs often by prearrangement, as in discussion following lectures and debates. The resister, whether vocal or silent, is an essential participant.

Form C is quite common, especially at sewing circles and all that sort of thing. Forms A and C are often difficult to distinguish. Participants themselves seldom know which form is being practiced.

Form D is all too rare. It calls for craftsmanship. It is itself an art, and its practice develops breadth of mind, poise and sapiency.

XXIV

Passing the Buck

THERE are two divisions into which, at this meditative moment, I am tempted to put all young people. The first contains those who can be their natural selves when in the company of adults; the second, those who can not. The first are those who, allowing for varying degrees of shyness, chat naturally and companionably with people of advanced years, recognizing in them potential comrades and friends. The second group is an armed camp, with entrenchments and sentries. Any adult is an enemy, trained to use force of arms, spies, chaperons, parental authority and other weapons of war. They see the necessity of conversation with such a foe now and then, during a sort of truce, but throughout they will be stilted, unduly formal, or betray somehow a vague ill-will.

As a teacher whose lot now is cast in pleasant places it is my fortune to meet young people of the first group. But recent contacts here and there make me suspect that the second division gains enough recruits to balance desertions from its ranks. I should like to believe that this is not true, for if Youth and Age be friends and allies, humanity can step forward more briskly.

Every teacher knows the pleasure of dealing with those students who meet him on terms of a common experience, common vocabulary, and as associates on a common quest. And every teacher knows the benumbing experience of facing a pupil whose real self he cannot reach. There are no thoughts in common; no experiences, almost no common vocabulary. Groping then for the *argot* of his own youth he tries to approach, feeling all the time like a herald parleying with a foe who considers his foreign accent absurd.

It is a truism to say that boys and girls of a generation ago were at home during more hours out of the average twenty-four, and more days out of the year than they are now. Just because there was less to do outside the home, they or their parents had to invent more things to do inside it. There were no motor cars, no movies, no summer "camps"; and less deliberate segregation of the young. Undoubtedly the old folks, too, had less chance to gad about.

In those hours which the family of necessity spent together, some things were invented to make the time pass, some things were demanded by parents because of convictions or conventions that are dying out. There was more reading aloud by one of the elders. Whatever reading a boy might choose for himself, the books he heard read aloud were ones that brought old and young together in intellectual or emotional sympathy, and provided a common vocabulary.

There was more table conversation, because the entire family came together more often at meal-times. Not that there was less family nagging and bickering —among brothers and sisters even that may contribute to the socializing process—but there was more time for something else, such as comments on the news of the day, and discussions of neighborhood happenings from older as well as younger viewpoints.

There were family games—"we were happy because we played Halma." There was candy making of a Sunday afternoon in the kitchen when the cook was out. More often than today was there a cook who tolerated experiments in her sanctuary. Mother and daughter had more time to practice together household management. Boys had more time at home to put up a shelf or tinker with a broken lock.

The task of the school teacher was then simple enough,—a few branches of learning, and ability to impart that knowledge. There was classroom discipline; the rest of the schooling came from merely letting pupils run with their fellows. They came to school with a knowledge of their parents' ideas on many subjects; a large working vocabulary, which meant words to think with; and practical knowledge of such problems as arise in the home laboratory.

It is impossible to guess when any change first began in this balance between the functions of home and school. But just as soon as any fair proportion of pupils come to school without such background, the school must begin to provide it as well as it can. Each classroom must adopt a vocabulary that can be understood by all who are in it; each teacher must move the beginning of his story back to the point where the least coöperating home quit work. When households began to send daughters to school without a rudimentary experience in cooking, the demand arose for the schools to provide it. When a considerable group of boys began to arrive at school without having learned to be handy with their hands, the school had to begin to take up that training as well.

There are some who see nothing in this to complain about. Having Government do for us many of the things that individuals once did for themselves is the same as having the school do much that the home once did.

But there are serious complaints today of "the rising costs of education." In many states, even before the depression, public schools were rapidly approaching the limit of state solvency. What is the use of protesting? Children are crowding in from every type of household. At one extreme are those homes which could never offer any sort of laboratory as efficient as that of the school. At the other extreme are those which are glad to be spared the bother of child training in any field. The school, in the face of such widely exercised pressure, cannot lay down any burden it has once assumed.

So college teachers are complaining that boys and girls come to them in increasing numbers "without enough background." When they say this they do not mean that these youngsters are badly prepared in algebra or Latin. They mean that there is a lack of general knowledge, a poor vocabulary, a juvenile viewpoint toward all human problems,—an actual lack of *common sense*. They may easily have more knowledge than their teachers possess in a few narrow fields; they may know all about the entrails of an automobile, or the antennæ of a wireless outfit; and their limited vocabularies may contain many esoteric words. But ask business men today if they are content with the product of public school plus business college, minus background. Even perfection in spelling and punctuation, and a marvelous finger-speed upon the keyboard cannot compensate for certain arid spaces in the mind.

The world seems to be saying to the colleges today: "You are teaching these young people everything but horse-sense." The colleges reply, "See what the schools are sending us!" And the school says, "We had them only five hours out of the twenty-four, and five days out of the seven, and (what with vacations) only a tenth of the hours in the year. We can't move them forward very far in that time, if they are allowed all of the other nine-tenths in which to slip back. The home is shirking." And the home says to the school, "What are we hiring you for?" This, in the language of the day, is called Passing the Buck.

It would seem that the home has transferred certain tasks that the school cannot perform nearly so well, if at all. And by reason of transferring them it has ceased to be the sort of home that can perform them, so it cannot take them back again. Nor can the school perform its original tasks quite so well because of this additional burden. And there you are!

The entrenched young folks in that great second division of mine come from wealthy homes as often as from poor ones. Some elegant finishing schools are breeding places for them. I am thinking at this moment of a sixteen-year-old in a hotel reception room. There had been no earlier crossing of our paths in any way; yet I found myself wondering what I could have done to deserve the antagonism that was so apparent. It was only after I had heard other grown-ups refer to her as sullen or impudent, that I found myself coming to her defense. She was merely armed, with sentries on the watch at every point of approach. Her home experience either provided no adult comrades or else home had altogether ceased to be. In the sort of school she attended the teacher stayed in one camp and she in another, enemies, each seeking by force or strategy to gain an advantage in the battle.

As a teacher, I think that the answer to it all lies in the home. There are some responsibilities that cannot be transferred. It is true enough that all through the ranks of teaching, in public and private schools and in colleges, there are those grown-ups who offer opportunities for comradeship between youth and age that must cause many desertions from youth's armed camp. But teachers deal with youth *en masse*. Grown-ups in the home deal with them one at a time, or in little groups, with in-born affection as a powerful ally.

The home has passed the buck to the schools, but teachers are passing it back again, and there it must stay. Unless we want to communize our children the home has got to get back on the job.

XXV

Teachers at Bay

I HAVE nailed together some boards to make a book-case. There is the business of sandpapering, and some gingerbread work at the corners, and putty here and there, and then the paint carefully over all. As the work progresses, crude as it may be, I find a sort of fever possessing me to get it done. When the creation finally stands there in all its questionable perfection, I stand and look at it. I stroll away, to come back and look at it again. If it has taken me until bedtime I find that I want to get out of bed, walk across the cold floor, turn on the light and look at it once more—lingeringly. And then I am through! I shall hardly notice again whether it is of tin or mahogany so long as it holds the books up. But that fever of creating, and those moments of gaining from the sight of it a thrill of accomplishment have been adequate reward. Pretty soon I shall want to make another.

There is the same satisfaction to be had from the

contriving of any little thing with a pocket knife; not merely to whittle, but to shape a piece of wood into some little doo-dad that never existed before. No matter how insignificant the objective, there is still that same fever to get it done and that same momentary thrill of contemplation; then it may be just as well to throw it away.

The discovery of an argument for a sonnet tucked away somewhere in my mind sets the pulse to beating in that same fashion, intensifying steadily as I grope for the right words and arrange them in happy adjustment to the rhythm and the thought; then comes the warm glow of satisfaction over accomplishment. One may read such a thing over several times, not critically but contentedly. Then if he is lucky he forgets it. Later still, and quite apart, may come a fit of depression and self-distrust, like a chill after fever. But that is a matter of individual temperament.

Any effort to analyze the creative processes is business for the psychologist. But I believe that the artist who is a part of us all, whether we be cooks or gardeners or engineers, goes through these same experiences and enjoys the same rewards. They are not measured in terms of the world's appreciation, but by the artist's own eagerness in effort, and pleasure in the relaxed contemplation after strain. And I have a notion that there is this same thrill and the same sort of reward to be had from teaching.

Educators just now are bandying the word "creative" about, and either it does not mean anything at all as they use it, or it means too many things. They talk of "creative teaching" and mean only that something has been created in the minds of students. But any pupil may manage to build for himself out of crude material a new idea or a new dream; and he may have done all of the creative work himself with an automaton behind the teacher's desk. He has been a creative learner.

Teaching is a creative art only if that impulse toward creativity is present in the teacher, with the fever of effort to accomplish something, and the thrill when something seems to have been accomplished.

What is the "something" that I seek to create in one of my students? Certainly not a walking catalogue of facts, or a calculating machine, or a robot that can perform one particular task with painful exactitude. As I come to know men and women who seem well educated, I find this definition growing in my mind: a daring and insatiable curiosity about the truth; an ability and a willingness to follow any line of thought to some conclusion; an acquired technique of accomplishment; finally, tolerance toward others and a sense

of responsibility for one's own full share in our democratic experiment. What I want to see growing before
my eyes, then, is a purpose, and a way of using the
mind.

There may be many other things that a teacher
might seek; things related to morals, for instance, or
manners. If it is my business to impart wisdom or
morals, then I fear I shall have to take time off, to
increase my own stock-in-trade. But I might set these
youngsters to studying the pages of history, or experi-
menting in a laboratory, or practicing written composition, and be so conscious of the objective which I have
just defined that I could work along with them enjoying the thrill of creation.

One who pretends to teach must keep attending to
his own education, using his own definition for it. So
in these pages I have been setting myself small tasks;
whether thoughts beckon me gravely or gayly I must
follow them to a conclusion. I must do my own thinking, questioning all axioms and such-like short cuts,
however elementary my processes may be. In my
teaching I must challenge all routine; avoiding it sometimes for no reason at all other than the good of my
soul. For when a teacher's work becomes routined the
creative spirit dies. Two thousand years ago an old
Roman remarked, "Repetition, like rehashed cabbage,

kills the school-masters." There were some surprisingly wise old fellows who lived in that far-off day.

Holding fast to these notions, there are many times when I find myself a professor at bay. First, when I come into conflict with established routines; not my own, but those established long ago by others, and now possessing the sanctity of custom. Second, when I find myself engaged in the business of education *en masse*.

A perfect piece of educational machinery is set up whenever a youth and an older man walk and talk and work together. The youth provides eager inquiry, a willingness to abandon the restraints of the past, and a readiness to adventure into the unknown upon a basis of untested hypotheses. The older man offers experience, the products of mental speculation, a respect for tested tradition, and a technique which may avoid needless error and prevent waste of time.

When this machinery is expanded, and we have one man talking and working with ten youths, and attempting to pass along his experience to each one, something is lost. But when we have five hundred men attempting all at the same time to do it with five thousand youths, it seems as though the machinery must break down. There are so many necessary adjustments which have nothing to do with education,—conflicts of schedule, social problems among the five thousand who have to be brought together and regimented, loss of a sense of intimate companionship, and a hundred other things which seem to drain the oil from the machine, and put sand in its place.

When I try to determine the desired result of composition courses, for instance, and then to propose how that result may best be attained, my reasoning is forever being distorted by a consciousness of the unwieldy engine which must be used. My imagination is put under restraint, my hopes are curtailed, and I think only of the highest result that might possibly be attained for the crowd as a whole.

These should be troubles enough. But an artist likes to work quietly, the turmoil and excitement only within his own breast. If that morsel of me which is artist finds itself beset not only by the clamor of the campus, but by the voices of press, pulpit and public, all advising, admonishing or forbidding, then I am indeed at bay.

XXVI

Campus against Classroom

I AM a teacher in the new world, where a common school education for all and a higher education for any is axiomatic. But we have repeated the axiom so often that we have forgotten what its words mean,—especially "education."

Old World universities began as nothing more than groups of teachers who taught wherever they happened to be: around them gathered students from near and far who cared to listen and question. When a student thought he had gotten all he could, he went away and sat at the feet of some one else. Students also lived as and where they chose, though with the clannishness of youth they often flocked toward some one quarter of the town. Teachers who had nothing to offer got no students, and obviously had to shut up shop. There was no tenure of service for them.

Then came the New World. The state saw its moral duty clear to send all of its youth to school, and offer a "higher" education for those planning to preach. College authorities were made responsible for the behavior of students who had been taken from the care of parents and pastors and must be protected from the snares of the world while preparing for the Christian ministry.

The American college took students into residence and was from the start bicameral, like the new American congress. It had two chambers, Campus and Classroom, and its founders intended that these should work together toward one end.

There was no question about the end. The curriculum trained for the ministry, and all teaching and all campus living must be orthodox. President Thomas Clap of Yale wrote in 1754, "Colleges are Societies of Ministers for Training up Persons for the Work of the Ministry." This model set by Harvard, Yale, William and Mary, and others in the van, influenced all later colleges in this new world. Dartmouth was founded in 1769 to train missionaries for the Indians; Amherst in 1821 for "the education of indigent young men with the ministry in view." Union College, founded in 1795, was unique in that its founders represented no one creed or sect. In a Carnegie Report issued in 1907 five hundred and nine colleges out of seven hundred were found to be still under denominational control, though their own administrators generally admitted this was of small advantage, either educationally or morally. The pattern had been followed as the frontier moved westward, and sects followed the frontier, and colleges were seeded by the sects. Mission colleges were planted by one denomination within a stone's throw of those planted by another, for devoted leaders sometimes worked harder for the glory of their sects than for the glory of God; and immediately these self-styled "Christian colleges" entered into a most unchristian competition for students.

The first graduates were trained by Campus and Classroom while the two had unity of purpose. The Campus successfully kept them loyal to the church. Its prayer-meetings, revival services, debating societies, and compulsory chapel harmonized with a classroom which sought first of all to sustain the old theology, and adapt science to religion. Only twenty years ago, and even more recently, it was possible to find such phrases as these in college catalogues: "The biology taught at X University has no sympathy with that evolutionary theory that makes man the offspring of the animal"; "The History of Education is traced from its origin in the Garden of Eden"; "Science is esteemed because science was to Daniel the handmaid of his religion."

Very early in the life of our colleges the classroom was deflected from its original purpose. The true teacher, brought to a faculty because of devotion to his subject, began to seek scholarship first and the good of the church second. Then, as the colleges grew, students came from outside the sectarian fold and managed to graduate in a state of sin. To take care of increasing numbers, the college welcomed outside support. The denomination was no longer the dictator. Teachers gained new freedom to urge scholarship for its own sake, and influential graduates and friends, wise and unwise, began to express their views as to what the curriculum should contain and how it should be taught.

At the same time even more radical changes occurred within the Campus. Students, required to live together so that they might be more easily "protected," were developing a campus life of their own which was like nothing else on earth. "Activities" began to emerge —games played outside; glee clubs and debaters that traveled; worldly-minded newspapers and magazines. Clubs were formed and, following the Masonic model, were bound together by secret oaths and rituals. Worldly dances forced their way in, despite the frowns of trustees. All these things grew up spontaneously, independent of the classroom and indifferent to it, though not at first antagonistic. But they made the Campus forget its original purpose.

Next came the most interesting phenomenon in all our educational picture. Alumni were going forth from the colleges who were trained by the Campus and *not* by the Classroom; and well trained, at that. Four years of enforced association with companions of their own age developed at best a skill in leadership, and at the least a knowledge of how to get along with other men. Corners were rubbed off and practical skills developed which would make for business success. Of course the Classroom strove to place its imprint upon these undergraduates, but Youth developed a fine technique of evasion. For the Classroom was governed by gentle scholars devoted to their own subjects and ready to assume an equal devotion on the part of neophytes. Of course there were always students who were being trained solely by the Classroom, but they were set apart from the others as "greasy grinds"; it was the Campus-graduate who began to determine America's popular definition of what "college" meant. If after graduation he became the patron of the college it is no wonder that his first impulse was to build a stadium and make his dollars and his influence felt more in support of the Campus than of the Classroom of the future.

The old unifying objective had gone. The Classroom

found itself preparing young men and women for every sort of worldly activity, and groping professors tried to provide by "electives" a curriculum that would suit them all, and outwit the shrewd young evader by perplexing systems of "credits" and "cuts" and other machinery. The Campus, also having lost its aim, began to seek another within itself. The two chambers were growing rapidly away from one another, and without singleness of purpose and mutual support each was ripe for exploitation.

Such large groups of young people could not be overlooked for long by eager exploiters. Efforts to pervert the Classroom came from many directions. The scholarly professor wishes to show his students *how* to think. The exploiter wishes them told *what* to think. Political parties naturally wanted to control teachers who had so great an opportunity to influence young voters. Not many years ago in the south and west there were instances of an entire faculty being dismissed and replaced by one of different political complexion. High protectionists, prohibitionists, antivivisectionists, feminists, anti-vaccinationists, proponents of birth control or a soviet form of government each in its turn sought to win the allegiance of teachers and direct their teaching; and the parent denomination always felt it had an inherent right to control teaching.

Perhaps the most confused and confusing disturbance has been the effort of graduates to prevent "false teaching." One group might insist that professors could not teach the truth because they were muzzled by a capitalistic board of trustees; another, that all college faculties are hotbeds of dangerous radicalism. Some were incensed because the theology of an earlier generation was not forced upon the undergraduate in the classroom; others protested that an outworn belief was handicapping educational progress.

But the steadiest pressure came from those graduates of the Campus who, having succeeded in the world, wanted the Classroom to become less scholarly and more practical-minded, applying itself directly to the current techniques of commerce.

As these various efforts increased, the Classroom developed greater resistance, because it never lacked either dignity or self-respect. Eventually it took measures to protect itself, and a nation-wide association of professors came into being to establish the right of teachers to seek truth without fear or favor. But while the groping work of this association and a clearer understanding of the problem by administrators have done much to protect the Classroom, it is still difficult to resist the pressure of any alumni group, in an endowed college which recognizes their loyalty and seeks their financial support; or of sectarian leaders where the college is still controlled by a sect, or of politicians where it is controlled by a legislature.

All of these forces which have attempted to exploit the Classroom have turned more hungrily toward the throngs of young people when they were outside the Classroom doors, and easier to manipulate.

First, the propagandist! It is of small importance to him that his efforts might confuse or obstruct teaching. Militarists, protesting that pacifism held the faculty in its clammy grip, send their own organizers to arouse student emotions and secure their allegiance. Pacifists, equally certain that militarism, uniformed as a Reserve Officers Training Corps, is working its will with the college, do their own sapping and mining. Parsons and agnostics, radicals and rotarians have seen their duty clear. The worst legacy left the colleges after wartime years was the habit of intensive drives for student funds. It does not take great organizing skill to arouse the mass emotion of a throng of students; nor is it so hard to persuade many of them to pledge money which their fathers provide. Every sort of organization just after those years fought for its "tag day," and resistance on the part of worried administrators often led to an unfair accusation of lack of sympathy with the Cause.

Efforts to exploit the Campus by emotional groups of its own graduates form a greater problem. The "hippodroming" of student games for the entertainment of graduates and public need not be discussed here in detail; much has already been written about it. Colleges and universities here and there have been cleaning house, and some have tried to make a thorough job of it. But many houses thus cleaned have been soiled again by alumni who insist upon winning teams. Universities announce officially, for instance, that free board is no longer provided members of the team in return for their playing. And immediately certain alumni come forward who quietly pay out of their own pockets the board bill of players. Such graduates pay the expenses of promising athletes even in high school, until these youngsters brazenly offer themselves to the highest bidder.

Efforts to improve the athletic situation, especially after the "Carnegie Report," seemed to be effective until the depression came along. Then gate receipts suddenly became of greater importance, and universities whose teams played the "big-time circuits" slipped back to a worse condition than before. Some harassed educators have even proposed that it might be just as well to pay all players for their labors, just as other campus employees are paid, and so get rid of the whole perplexing problem. And it is perplexing. Now and then some small college which has no business in the picture pokes its head suddenly above the athletic horizon, having—as one sports-writer gayly phrased it—"gone out an' hired 'emselves a big team." I have in mind the record of a boy in a well-known eastern "prep" school who played outstanding football and so quite naturally wanted to know what X University would offer him. He was told that X was well supplied with quarterback material for the coming fall, but that if he would linger on in his prep school for one more year, his *school* tuition would be paid. He accepted the offer, and has entered X this year.

Not as much has been written about the exploitation of undergraduate clubs by Campus-graduates. The national fraternities demand allegiance from local chapters, which they themselves may have planted on a campus already well enough supplied. Most national organizations maintain headquarters with a traveling secretary, and publish a magazine. Nine-tenths of the cost of this graduate superstructure is borne by the undergraduate. He must make his remittance to national headquarters even though the taxes upon his local clubhouse are overdue, bills for furnishings are

unpaid, and the members of the club are largely engaged in hard labor outside of classroom hours in order
to pay their bills. Yet if he becomes restive under that
burden he must face the discipline of graduates whose
friendliness is now a vital necessity. What the undergraduates get from national headquarters in return for
their money is of course debatable and varies with the
group. But questions addressed to widely scattered students have brought the reply, "Little or nothing! A
semi-occasional visit from some representative whose
salary and traveling expenses we pay, who attempts in
a day's visit to acquaint himself with our problems and
help us solve them. His advice is never as sound as that
of any one of a dozen friendly faculty members or
neighboring business men, willing and able to serve us
in the same way; and he generally comes after we are
in trouble and not before." If the thousands in chapter
taxes which are paid to national headquarters were used
locally to repair chapter houses or paid into college
treasuries as campus taxes, only a few adults at national
headquarters would be the losers.

There are approximately two hundred and sixty-
three magazines, mostly quarterlies, published by the
national fraternities, sororities, and campus societies in
this country. Their annual cost aggregates more than a
million dollars and, generally speaking, they are not

read. Now and then a fraternity publication raises its head higher than the generality, by the accident of having a competent editor willing to sell his time in that way, but it drops back again.

Fraternity houses on American campuses, which in 1930 had an estimated value of ninety million dollars, are presenting their own problem with redoubled force since the depression. The building of many of them (so says the National Interfraternity Council) was encouraged by architects and contractors at a time when costs were lower, and when the undergraduate's spending money was not diverted by motor cars and off-campus movies; and they now ride upon his back like an old man of the sea. But it is in connection with exploitation of the undergraduates by the alumni that I mention them now, although many a graduate would ruefully insist that they have brought about an exploitation of the alumni by the undergraduates.

The young graduate returning to the Campus, looking forward to a renewal of college experiences without accompanying responsibilities, makes the "house" his headquarters. Because of his dignity as a graduate and his actual proprietary right, the undergraduate hesitates to enforce house rules against him. He can go drunk to the dances, take his own women friends, "stage a party" in an upstairs room, or set up a bar in the basement; and it is difficult for student house committees to expel him, even if they are not induced to join in. From the old New England college to the Pacific Coast university comes the same testimony from men who are concerned: "The boys are doing their best to solve these fraternity questions, but they cannot handle the young graduate."

The final exploiter of the Campus has been a certain type of business man. Nearly every undergraduate activity is a purchaser of goods or services, and it is surprising how much money can be raised from even poverty-stricken students.

"Honorary" societies, which choose their membership from leaders of the Campus rather than the Classroom, spend money on pins and programs, food and orchestras. Imitating the older social and scholarship fraternities, they link up with their kind in other colleges, and a single campus may have dozens, most of them started from without. It is even possible for a second honorary society to be formed in a field already occupied, so that students not honored by election to one may be chosen by their friends in another. One case may serve to illustrate the type. Students in a large university engaged in the editing of a campus publication were urged to form a local chapter of a new honorary society for senior editors and business managers. A printed constitution and by-laws and ritual for initiation were all provided, and dues specified. Each member would be privileged to wear the pin of the national organization and receive free a copy of the society's magazine devoted to bigger and better publications of this sort. The initiation fees were $10.00 per student, $8.00 of which was to go to the national headquarters! If only five students were secured, that would mean $40.00 to be sent to a gentleman in the middle west. If he could establish one hundred chapters among the six or seven hundred colleges in the land whose students bring out such publications, that would be $4000 annually for letter paper and traveling expenses at the national headquarters, and something over. Inquiries sent to the citizens of the town where these "national headquarters" were located revealed that the new honorary society was the private enterprise of a young business man, who operated alone.

Some campuses have enough honorary societies and clubs to provide a gold badge for every senior student wanting such an honor without overcrowding any single society. In one university I have counted sixty. Naturally the makers of fraternity pins are interested. Why not? If it is worth while for greeting-card manufacturers to invent a Father's Day and endeavor to legislate in favor of more kindly feelings toward father throughout the land, it is certainly worth while for jewelers and engravers to stimulate honorary societies in several hundred colleges, not to mention several thousand high schools. In an eastern university where half of the students are trying to earn their way, ten thousand dollars are collected annually in club dues and five thousand of this is sent to distant "headquarters."

The profiteer finds other and more fruitful campus contacts. Student social affairs undertaken on a large scale, because each new group of students wishes to surpass its predecessors or some sister university, often have surprisingly large sums at their disposal. A "junior prom" committee, for instance, may be able to spend a thousand dollars for an orchestra and other thousands for decorations, refreshments, programs, and favors. If the committee has been selected, not because of outstanding good taste and business judgment, but through campus politics, it falls an easier prey to the outside exploiter. Engravers are prepared to offer the student in charge of programs a substantial fee for his own private pocket in exchange for the contract. Decorators, orchestras, caterers have all been made familiar with this way of doing business with undergraduate committees. Such conditions have continued in certain universities visited year after year by the same traveling salesmen for these wares. Yet student personnel has changed each year. This leads to the inference that the vicious custom is kept alive largely by the outside business man rather than the student. Testimony from advisers of students in different universities reports the same technique. Generally there is a dual billing for the goods received. One bill for services or commodities is sent to the student manager for him to pay, and another for him to file with the "faculty adviser" or auditing committee. Or else the student manager, in return for awarding the contract, is offered agency work in his spare time among other colleges or neighboring high schools; and he is promised some advance on account of future commissions.

The publishing of college annuals is a $2,500,000 business throughout American colleges, with as much again spent by high school seniors throughout the country. One western State university spent $25,000 annually on its book; another $35,000. An inexperienced boy may find himself, as manager of the annual, handling a budget of $10,000 or $12,000 and trying to fight off the propositions made to him by photographers, engravers, printers, or binders; or made to him by men who do none of these things, but set themselves up as "builders of college annuals," secure the contract, and then farm out the different processes wherever they like. So important has this business become that the American Typothetae, or national organization of employing printers, set up a distinct informational division in its Washington offices known as the Printers of College Annuals.

Some other campus publications offer as much food for thought. The sudden increase after the war in the number of campus "comics" was due not so much to the spontaneous desire of students suddenly to burst into humorous prose and verse, but to the energy of one national magazine whose publisher testified in court proceedings that he had started at least fifty of these magazines, subsidizing each one after creating it, making it a subscription solicitor, and retaining exclusive right to reprint its jokes.

The development of all sorts of campus publications into a large business in the aggregate has led to the organization of advertising agencies or "counselors" who handle the college accounts of national advertisers, and parcel the contracts out, retaining 35 per cent for themselves and a second agent.

Have I painted too gloomy a picture? Yes, so far as some institutions are concerned. College executives when asked today about campus conditions answer that such abuses belong to the past. But do they always know? One writes that bad financial management of

undergraduate organizations was ended long ago by
the setting up of "compulsory auditing." Yet on that
campus a student manager in the same year sold the
right of succession to a student in the following class
for three hundred dollars. An Assistant to the President writes from another university that the student
magazine has had a worthy and unbroken record for
many years, "wholly under student control"; and a
dean of the same institution testifies that it had become
insolvent three years before, had been granted financial
aid, and might not be allowed to continue another
year because of bad management. An executive of another institution, asked to make some sort of apology
for legally libelous matter appearing in a publication
bearing the university name wrote that it is "wholly
under student control," and that he supposed "no one
ever took notice of matter appearing in student publications." In the effort to avoid loose assertions I have
made many inquiries of concerns dealing with undergraduates. One that I most recently addressed boasts a
nation-wide service to college customers. The reply ex-
pressed regret that such methods of doing business were
undoubtedly general and complained, incidentally, of
their great expense. It urged that more attention be
paid by authorities in the colleges to these student affairs; and the letter ended by offering a ten per cent

commission to the *college official* who would get them a student contract!

As a result of all this exploitation the campus is in danger of losing whatever coherency it ever possessed. Instead of working in collaboration with the classroom, it turns against it, robbing it of time for study and time for profitable leisure.

The average number of weeks in an academic year is only thirty-two. Because we "educate" our youngsters wholesale, the machinery for enrolling and examining them is cumbersome at best. In the average large university a week and a half are spent getting ready at the beginning of the year; another two weeks are lost in the middle, getting ready for "mid-year" examinations and getting over them; and another week and a half at the end—five weeks, or nearly one sixth, taken from the Classroom for the business of organization and tests.

Then come the demands of the Campus. The freshman who is going to join a fraternity must surrender precious hours to the clap-trap of initiation. "Hellweek" is a well-named period of nerve strain that for eight or ten days makes the freshman "pledge" unfit for class work, and demands almost as much from the older students who initiate him. The athletic schedule offers outstanding games which upset class programs, with a day or two of preparation and a day to recover. "Proms" with attendant "house parties" do not mean an evening dance after the day's work is over. They mean at least one day gone clean out of the schedule for a surprising number of students, and many days of preparation for every one who takes any part in arranging the affair. In many colleges "senior week" or "junior week" is a fixture with festivities supplanting study for five or six consecutive days.

These fixed hours which the Campus steals from the Classroom are easy to count. The theft is so well grounded on tradition that the Classroom meekly surrenders them as a matter of course. It even allows, in most colleges, a fixed number of "cuts" or unexplained and excused absences to provide for emergency. These the average student uses up at once as a matter of conscience, thus throwing away the equivalent of another week.

But there is more than theft of time. The Campus has been at war with scholarship. First, there is the strain caused by all of these activities, all the time, upon the minds and nerves of all who take part in them. Every teacher who becomes intimately acquainted with his students is familiar with the emotional outburst of the senior who says, "If only I could begin it again, I should leave out nine-tenths of the activities. I have just begun to get interested in this or that course, and I haven't the time to do it justice." Or the young woman who says, "I should like to do something worth while in the really important business of college, but every moment outside the Classroom is absorbed by committee work or claimed by my sorority. I must go there, if only to shed sweetness and light on the freshmen, who also are being kept away from work in order to develop a spirit of comradeship in the sisterhood. I am working my way through college. Every time the sorority has a dance and I am taxed a few dollars it means not only that I must give time to help get the house ready and then go to the party, but I must work a dozen hours outside, washing some one's baby to earn the tax which I am paying." Multiply this several times over throughout the academic year to gain an idea of its importance.

In this war of the Campus against the Classroom, the larger universities have been the battlefields. When one estimates the number of weeks of actual classroom work in the academic year, and what the student pays for them, one realizes the drain of prolonged trips by any student organizations in term time. An eastern college famous for its athletic teams has boasted in its publicity that its football players will travel seven thousand miles in the coming season. Moreover, the player who is essential to the team if it is to win games must not be allowed to get below grade and become ineligible. There is more pressure upon the teacher than even he is generally willing to admit to force him to give passing marks to the star athlete and to ignore absences due to extra training and games away from home.

The attack of the fraternity is not so well-defined. It takes the form of a conflicting allegiance. Even a young man cannot serve two masters. Reports read at the national meeting of the Interfraternity Council state specifically that the low scholarship record of fraternity men is due to their prevailing habit of staying away from classes for no reason at all other than to "sit around" in the house.

During the past fifty years of fraternity existence these clubs have spurred their young members on to seek preëminence, it is true, but on the Campus rather than in the Classroom. So great did their power at one time become that they selected trustees and set up and dethroned college presidents. During the past few years the Classroom has been gaining in courage to fight back, and has forced the publication of relative scholastic standing among the fraternities. They accepted the innovation grudgingly at first, but now generally face it as inevitable. Yet it does not wholly change the picture. Just as the athlete has demanded passing grades to keep him eligible, so the fraternity member demands them to keep his own brotherhood from the bottom of the list. American college faculties find themselves worrying about the tendency of their students to seek marks rather than an education, and they struggle to find devices for overcoming this evil. Yet all the forces which brought it about continue to exert pressure.

The fraternities and sororities have not only been at war with the Classroom, but they have fought among themselves in a competitive seeking after campus honors. This has led to an imitation of some of the worst features of outside political trickery; the substitution of skill in vote-getting for actual worth, in the awarding of campus distinctions, has harmed the morale of Campus and Classroom alike.

The Campus deals its final blow at the Classroom when it diverts the attention of teaching experts from the tasks for which they are best fitted and drafts them for service on athletic committees, dance committees, publication boards, and disciplinary courts to deal with drunkenness, secret marriage, or "over-cutting" of classes. In forcing college teachers to spend some of their time as nurses it has forced the college student back toward the nursery. The Old World university matured its students. The American campus has invited immaturity and prolonged it.

What is the campus? Let a teacher answer whose fantastic hope it was that young people would some day come to college to train their minds by planned work and productive leisure. It is a thief of time! It has become a confusion of noise and motion. Activities which began as spontaneous outlets for natural energy have jelled into conventional forms. Athletic teams engaged in intercollegiate games and far travel; glee clubs; choruses; orchestras; dramatic troupes; debating teams; magazines; newspapers; year-books; fraternities; sororities; honorary societies; clubs, clubs, and yet more clubs; campus politics; class organizations; dance committees; all of these are the campus. Just what is it? Nobody knows. Flattered, misled, and spanked in turn, it has become at times assertive and at times resentful. Administrators, perplexed by its vagaries, have sometimes turned their backs upon it, and sometimes have resorted to increased policing, with compulsory audits, graduate managers, and a confusion of rules.

An educator from Mars visiting an American university would be surprised to discover that in one part of the institution classes were conducted in accounting, while in another part inexperienced students were handling large amounts of money with resultant mistakes, humiliations, and petty peculations due to lack of advisors, badly kept books, or no books at all. He would find classrooms studying the history of the press, its ethical code, and practice in newspaper ways of writing; and outside the classroom, publications edited and written by students who not only lacked such classroom training but earnestly avoided it. He would find an active Campus experimentation in many fields which might be helped by the Classroom and help it in turn, yet the Classroom is utterly indifferent to its existence. He would find sentimental administrators trying to justify the existence of the Campus as an educational factor by talking about "student self-government," and setting up in its name a system under which students are encouraged to make last year's mistakes all over again—mistakes which are ignored if they harm only the students, and punished if they affect the welfare of the corporate institution. He would find students who violated social rules given academic penalties, and students who failed to meet academic requirements given social punishment.

He might hear, as I did in a women's college, a student protesting, "I came here as the result of financial sacrifice, to spend four years under the direction of experts. A great deal of my time is wasted because a few inexperienced and excited girls want to try experiments in governing me. So far as I am concerned, the experts can be as arbitrary as they like, if I know they are expert!"

Where is the American Campus going? First, of course, wherever the Classroom goes. For good or ill, they are bound together. Unless they have a common objective they are sure to trip each other up. If they are brought into harmony it may be necessary to reshape the Classroom more than the Campus. For in the activities of the Campus, students at least know just why they are doing whatever they do, at the very moment of doing it; whereas there is a good deal of Classroom procedure which is unexplained or has no immediate value and offers only a vague future reward. And the Classroom itself does not now know whether it is aiming toward scholarship as an end, or toward citizenship, or toward fitness for a specific job, or merely toward "marks."

Campus and Classroom are, however, slowly acquiring a certain coördination, and it is generally small groups of alumni who are last to read the writing on the wall. Student dramatic organizations here and there which at one time bumbled along under student mismanagement, merge into the dramatic department, so that one can hardly tell where student-conducted activities end and curricular work begins. Glee club, choir and student band find expert faculty trainers. Debating carries its teams farther afield and interests a larger group of students than ever before, while the majority of teachers or students are unable to say where student initiative ends and faculty initiative begins, nor would they care. Athletics, and by that term is not meant the growing "intramural" structure, but all the energies focusing in intercollegiate games, have been transferred from the control of semi-independent athletic committees dominated by alumni to the central executive authority of the University, and coaches are not only members of the faculty but most of them render teaching service, in addition to the task of grooming university teams. Publications are moving more slowly toward the natural relationship which should exist between them and all "writing courses." Most slowly of all move the fraternities, and trailing them the string of so-called honorary societies with their heavy and useless superstructure. More than one university has taken over ownership of fraternity houses, and leased them to their student occupants. At one university students themselves suddenly wiped out a large number of worthless "societies," leaving one or two to afford their chosen members an actual distinction. Recent economic conditions have not been wholly harmful. Considerable chaff was blown from our campuses by the bitter winds of depression, and in a shorter time than some tired executives ever dreamed was possible.

No strictures in this article upon fraternities are half so severe as those which may be heard uttered by thoughtful men assembled at interfraternity councils; no comment upon the abuses of intercollegiate athletics so bitter, or upon honorary societies so cynical, as editorials which appear from day to day in the undergraduate press throughout the country.

There is only one place for the Campus to go, and that is into a merger: combining with the Classroom to form an undergraduate college whose every nerve and bone and sinew are coördinated for the training of cultured leaders in a democracy; where courses of study, whether relating to the wisdom of the past or the new knowledge of today, are all so organized as to apply to a responsive and responsible life now; and where all activities upon the campus are, in effect, laboratories for citizenship. Such a college, even though it be part of a larger university, should be small enough to make possible that intimacy between youth and age which is the corner-stone of education. Its educational program should be determined by those who do the teaching,—and if any are not competent to share such a responsibility, their place is in a degree factory and not in this college of my dream.

The teaching in such a college is not to be confused with that in a post-graduate school. Each instructor shares responsibility for far more than the transmitting of knowledge in his special field. He is constantly aware of Campus problems and his classroom shares in their solution. In expression of opinion he is free to follow where truth seems to lead, without opposition from any source, inside or outside the institution, so long as he evidently recognizes his full responsibilities in such a place. This is a harder task than post-graduate teaching, with more hours in its day, and a greater variety of tests to determine a man's fitness for it. But only such teachers can bring Campus and Classroom closer together; and our undergraduate colleges at their best can only muddle along until Campus and Classroom agree upon a desired result and then labor as one to attain it.

XXVII

The Garment of Learning

MANY years ago I heard Mr. William Dean Howells say, "I never find myself in a company of college-bred men without feeling that somehow I am not fully dressed." Mr. Howells possessed all those qualities of mind and spirit which one might seek as the perfect product of a college education,—tolerance, humor, faith in God and man, a disciplined power of thinking, and an unflagging curiosity. But he was sensitively aware of the fact that he never "went to college."

A similar remark was made to me by Mr. Dent, the great London publisher. I had seen him at a luncheon table facing the questions of a dozen experts representing different fields of university research, and answering each in the vocabulary of his kind, so that we all wondered at the breadth of his knowledge and understanding. After the luncheon, as we were walking away, he said, "I have had a lovely time, a lovely time!

But I never find myself in such company without wishing that I too were an educated man."

It is evident that I belong to an old and exclusive club. The membership is congenial, and I take as great a pleasure in it as ever I did. It is not really snobbish; but like other select societies it has acquired an *aura*. Outsiders peer curiously through this mist, sometimes with a jealous gaze, or with indifference, or with great respect, but not always discerningly. Because of this focused attention our members are prone to a certain self-consciousness, and the acceptance of prevailing notions about themselves. The club I refer to is the ancient and honorable company of College-Bred Men.

If Mr. Howells felt himself ill-dressed in a company of men like me, then we must indeed have created an illusion as to our sacrosanct membership; as though we, like the fox who lost his tail, had persuaded all of the other foxes to seek no further proof of our distinction. The allusion would of course apply better if the fox had had his tail draped in gown and hood.

But because of Mr. Howells and many others like him, I have often felt a certain humility at commencement time, when perfervid orators address me and my fellows as the very elect. I find myself gazing furtively about at the others, fearful that some one may betray me; and I wonder just what it was that happened during a certain four years when I was an unlicked cub, to transform me from common clay into the graceful and delicately tinted ornament I have become. Underneath it all is a sneaking suspicion that I am just the same old two-and-sixpence that I was before I went to college, polished in places, a little thinner from much circulation, and wiser in experience.

In fact a doubt is growing in my mind as to the soundness of much of the doctrine that is a part of our club code. There is for instance this common belief that college adds to a man more than he already has of native abilities. "It made us what we are today; it should be satisfied" is the chorus. Am I a traitor to the club if I assert that a college education really *adds* nothing at all to a man? If it is effective, it helps him to find and to organize what he has got. Aside from that I suspect there comes out of the mill exactly what went into it. If a young man is by nature a rascal it can not change him, but sends him forth an educated rascal, much more harmful to society for that reason.

If I am right, then a college owes the quality of its graduates very largely to the character of its subfreshmen. Assembled alumni should not so generally boast that Major General Howitzer graduated from dear old Siwash,—but rather that the General's shrewd old father had chosen it as the place for his boy. The more popular theory is harmless enough, except for this: it may lead a body of graduates to be over-fearful of changes in the conduct of the college that "made" them. It is a dangerous thing, they feel, to alter the machinery of creation. But if that machinery is not creative, but rather a cutting and polishing process, then it must be completely readjusted from time to time to fit changing types and generations of students. The diamond-cutters of Amsterdam could go far toward destroying a fine lump of coal.

Another current of opinion in our club has carried me along with it until I have suddenly found myself pausing to question. It is that the college owes a debt to its graduates which it must pay, and that the graduates owe a debt to the college.

What debt can a college possibly owe its graduates? Should it be grateful for the fame that comes to it by reason of their success in the world? That seems to me no debt at all. The worth of a college is measured by what it is now doing and can do; it must not busy itself about its past. Its business is the future, in peculiar measure.

What does it owe in return for material gifts? Colleges must have money, and bodies of alumni with their growing group-consciousness are generously and increasingly giving it.

Graduate generosity has various stimulants. To many a man, college symbolizes his own youth. He revisits the campus and lives again in spirit four years of irresponsible playtime, or regains some bit of youthful vision, and he is grateful for the rejuvenation. It offers to others an opportunity of allying themselves with some force that is making for the spiritual progress of the world. A man will often grope vaguely for such opportunities, until he suddenly discovers that his own college will actually claim him as closer than an ally in this cause,—almost a son in fact,—if he will but admit the tie. Another stimulant is still harder to define. Man craves immortality. If he himself cannot live on, he can at least become a part of something that will. So he gives of his substance to permanent foundations of all sorts. But if the college *turns aside* from its great business to do something for him in return, it ceases by just that much to justify his giving. It should not use its machinery for his comfort or benefit until it can show that it actually has surplus energy which is being wasted.

Any college may owe a debt to its graduates for the moral courage that comes from their loyalty and support. But that debt can be paid only by undeviatingly "carrying on."

It is a sentimental picture that reunion orators paint

of a three-fold army, faculty, students, and alumni, marching forward coöperatively together under one banner, whatever that banner may be, with the college president as leader. But there is something wrong with the picture. The college must march ahead, if it is to justify the support of its graduates; and even that much of an army under our American system too often kills its leader with overwork. If the graduates wish to organize, and by their combined encouragement urge the college on to a finer accomplishment, they must raise up their own organizers and leaders; and their generous giving of means and courage, and their congenial association with one another will bring their own sure reward. We college-bred men possess the power to urge our colleges on, and also the power to bother them greatly. It would be a pity if many of us came to feel that we could buy the right to be a bother!

I am honestly devoted to my ancient and honorable club. Its rooms are filled with good fellowship and happy reminiscence. But I think we do share a sort of masonic secret, and it is this: that some of us ought never to have gone to that sort of college, and others might better have gone to none at all. To many the experience meant only a wider circle of friends and acquaintances—it was no more than a house party. To some, it meant only the acquirement of bad habits of mind or manners. As for learning, some stared the sybil in the face and knew not what questions to ask; some never even saw her. To some she whispered, and the syllables continue to echo in their minds, and take on richer significance as time passes.

Gallia est omnia divisa enteuthen exalauni parasangas on auf hinter neben uber inter gaudiamus cum laude—which being interpreted, means "I too once reached out my hand hesitatingly—even reluctantly—and touched the hem of Learning's garment. Some virtue was transmitted, even in that brief contact; and emotions were stirred which have gained force with the years,—mingled longings and regrets—a respectful envy of true scholarship, and an honest humility in the presence of Learning."

XXVIII

Getting Educated Quick

A FEW years ago I visited a little western college that was undermanned and under-equipped, with not enough books in the library or chemicals in the laboratory, yet with a body of students so eager for an education that most of them got what they sought. One of the music staff had been invited to a famous eastern university, and I congratulated him on his promotion.

"You may call it that," he said mournfully, "but I'll never get such students again. During my years here," he went on, "I have had several students who came to me with diplomas in piano-playing conferred by a shoddy correspondence school, and not one of them had ever touched a piano! But to my surprise I found that each had gained something from those impersonal stereotyped lessons. I didn't have to begin at the beginning. They had managed to get some idea of the theory of harmony, some sense of the geography of the keyboard. During this past year I have given an hour every Sunday morning to the business of rearranging ten-finger exercises for the coming week into exercises for eight fingers, for a girl who has lost two fingers in farm machinery. She is bound to learn piano; when you hear her in recital this week, you won't suspect her handicap."

There are little colleges like that, in remote spots, lifted into dignity by students who demand an education and cannot afford to go further afield. Many of these colleges were founded by some religious denomination which succeeded in arousing enough enthusiasm among the faithful to start something, but not enough devotion to maintain it decently. Now they stand like broken promises in brick and stone; and a few of them are redeemed by their own students.

Several times I have been asked to meet a group of young people who formed the advertising staff of a large department store. They were not college trained, but had risen from the ranks of salesgirls and clerks. It was at their insistence that a college professor stole some of their outside time after a grinding day in the store. I found their questions had nothing to do with "shop"; they wanted to know what books to read, what to study, and whether there were any recipes for the writing of short stories and essays and verse. They were fighting for an education while they earned their living, and they seized upon any passing teacher. They were, in fact, drafting a faculty of their own, with such classroom hours as they could pick up here and there.

It is still a truism that more men have gained worldly success without a college education than with it. It must also be true that some men will acquire by their own unaided effort a portion of that grace we call scholarship.

In contrast to all this, I recall occasional attitudes of mind in my own undergraduate days in a little college that was well endowed; and I remember to my shame that it was possible for a young man to spend four years in that place and have the intellectual surfaces of his mind scarcely tickled. Lest this seem a reproach directed at one small New England college, let me add the testimony of a member of the Harvard faculty, who says that it was not until his senior year at Harvard that he found out where the library was, and then he hunted it down only because he had a sick room-mate who wanted a book. Times have changed a little. But our finest universities today are still granting diplomas to boys who paid a high price to get within reach of an education and then exercised marvelous ingenuity to avoid contact.

So what? I have seen men of cultivated mind who

never went to college; I have seen young people getting the best sort of educational experience out of a college that was miserably equipped; or even some education out of the multigraphed lessons of a shoddy correspondence school; and I have seen hundreds of youngsters wasting time at finely equipped universities, learning practically nothing except bad habits of work and play. Upon such data I must build my definition of *any* college, rich or poor; that it is *a place where the facilities for acquiring a higher education are conveniently assembled.* That is all; unless one adds, hopefully, *an atmosphere conducive to study.* The young man who elects to sit down in such an environment for four years may get up now and then to walk fifty feet in one direction to a library or one hundred yards in another direction to a laboratory; near him are pianos, and pictures, and experts on a lecture platform offering theories. By living there for four years he could easily condense into that period a rich educational experience that otherwise might take him half a lifetime to acquire. Or he might sit there for four years and go away in worse case than when he arrived. Perhaps the very ease of seeing the pictures or browsing among the books may lead him to undervalue them, to his life-long hurt; so that he will neither take what he finds at hand within college walls, or trouble to go further out into the world seeking it, as thousands of scholars have done who are brilliantly self-educated.

Mr. Howells and Mr. Dent shared a curious notion as to our colleges, a delusion which has flourished among all types of men and has filled the colleges to overflowing. It is not easy to condense that delusion into a single phrase, but it amounts to this: if a lad spends four years at college a mystery occurs, commonly described as "getting educated." This is presumably a sort of campus contagion, like the measles, which one acquires by being pleasantly exposed to it; and it leaves upon its victim a single beneficent pockmark known as a degree.

Once upon a time the demand for special skills far exceeded the supply. The boy who went to work at sixteen apprenticed to a vocation soon found so much employment for any knack, regardless of his mental equipment, that he often outstripped the one who had lingered for four years among books and theories and speculations and laboratory experiments. He could afford to jeer at a broader foundation of study.

But as competition became keener, the man who knew *how* but didn't know *why* began to find himself out-stripped even in his own craft by those who possessed broader vision and fertilized imaginations. Then he said to himself, "There must be something in this college business. I do not know just what it is, but I want my son to have it." From that vague moment until now, men of all sorts who have never gone to college have nursed the fancy that the college experience must *do* something to a boy and *tell* him something which forever set him apart; that "college-trained men" share some secret which no barbarian can possess. They are quite right. We graduates have the secret I have already divulged and I am a traitor to my cloth in revealing it. We alone know how true it is that one may spend four years on a college campus and be none the better for it; and that it is as easy to avoid acquiring real education there, as to acquire it.

This delusion that a college education is something which a college gives and a student receives has spread so far that even the colleges themselves seem to believe it. How else can one account for their pride as they point to outstanding statesmen and inventors and poets and scholars and say, "See what we did!" Without such a delusion they would say with more humility, "See what those men made of themselves! It is our good luck that they used us in the process." But perhaps the colleges are not wholly deluded. It may be necessary for them to nurse such a popular notion, so long as they are dependent upon the whim of legislators or the emotions of alumni for support.

When a public has come to believe that Education is something which is thrust upon its purchasers, other beliefs naturally follow. Any schooling must then be a series of recipes known to the elect,—the teachers. If they can be persuaded to tell, one is in a way to get educated. College Education must of course be something more. This the public vaguely defines as "instruction" plus "polish,"—both purchasable, and conveyed to any unresistant youth by experienced instructors and polishers.

"But," says the young man who cannot possibly afford four years of campus life, "if education is merely a series of secret recipes, why not buy them at once, and forego the polish, which, after all, is more of a luxury and seems to require more time?"

So he gropes questioningly about, and the answers shout back at him from billboards, and car-cards, and from the pages of every cheap magazine and some of the better ones. I quote from an advertising page in a single issue of a popular periodical:

LAW! LEARN AT HOME. Are you adult, alert, ambitious, willing to study? Investigate LAW! We guide you step by step—furnish all texts, including 14-Volume Law Library.

Training prepared by leading law professors and given by members of bar. Degree of LL.B. conferred. Low cost, easy terms. Send NOW for Free, 64-page "Law Training for Leadership."

BE A RAILWAY TRAFFIC INSPECTOR. Railway and Bus Lines Demand Men with this SPECIAL TRAINING. Active men—18 to 50—trained by our short, home-study course as Railway and Bus Passenger Traffic Inspectors advance quickly in this fascinating, healthful work. Travel or stay near home. Complete our training and we will place you at up to $140 per month, plus expenses, to start, or refund tuition.

FOLLOW THIS MAN! Secret Service Operator No. 38 is on the job! Running down dangerous Counterfeit Gang. Telltale fingerprints in murdered girl's room. FREE. The Confidential Report Operator No. 38 made to his chief. Write for it. EARN A REGULAR MONTHLY SALARY. You can become a Finger Print Expert at home, in your spare time, at small cost.

HOW DO YOU KNOW YOU CAN'T WRITE? Have you ever tried? Have you ever attempted even the least bit of training under competent guidance? Or have you been sitting back, as it is so easy to do, waiting for the day to come some time when you will awaken, all of a sudden, to the discovery, "I *am* a writer"? ......

BECOME AN EXPERT ACCOUNTANT. Executive Accountants and C.P.A.'s earn $3,000 to $15,000 a year. Thousands more are needed. We train you thoroughly at home in spare time for C.P.A. examinations or executive accounting positions. Previous bookkeeping knowledge or experience unnecessary.

USED CORRESPONDENCE COURSES and books sold or rented. Inexpensive. Money back agreement. Write for free catalogue. 4,000 bargains.

It is to the credit of us humans that we so yearn for accomplishment; even for accomplishments. I confess that my old heart beats a little faster when I read of the young man who couldn't contribute anything to the gayety of a party. Surely you have read his story? One evening a company of his friends had gathered, and some pretty girl said, "What can we do?" No one had a suggestion, and no one even dreamed of turning to him for an idea. Then nonchalantly he rose from his obscure corner and strolling over to the piano he sat down and played a bit of Chopin, and then a bit of Grieg, and then a popular waltz. All were entranced and amazed, until he explained that he had clipped a coupon and bought a course of lessons.

Even I, as I read it, begin to dream of the moment when I might suddenly step forward from my obscure corner at some dull faculty meeting, unlimber my accordion or my harmonica and soon have them all forgetting their misery and swaying to my magic strains.

Then there is the young man who at critical moments, when a persuasive voice was needed, always found himself tongue-tied. But after a short correspondence course in public speaking he was able to make a whole board of directors hang on his every word.

All of these appealing advertisements play upon a common human desire for accomplishment; and they are harmless if they imply merely that a skill may be acquired "well enough for practical purposes" by imitation. But they are vicious when they spread the delusion that education itself is but a series of recipes. "Train the mind, and it will eventually teach the hand to work its will" sounds like too slow a process for impatient youth. "Cultivate a skill, learn a formula or two, and the mind will take care of itself. That is the way to get educated quick."

These platitudes of mine would hardly be worth assembling if we had not just been through a financial depression. Our colleges were beginning to find out how to take care of the deluded;—the horde of those who arrived on a campus and then waited for a great educational change to occur; or those who dared the professors to learn 'em something.

But there are a thousand or so of undergraduate colleges and the struggle for existence among them is bitterly hard. They must maintain their enrollments. Many of them deserve credit because they will not lower the bars at entrance, even as a measure of self-preservation. But, whether they will admit it or not, they are eagerly profiting by the great delusion. "Enroll with us," they announce to willing listeners, "and we will teach you how, in thirty weeks."

Then begins the vicious circle. Young people who might once have looked forward to four years of contemplative study must now seek a practical training in the shortest possible time and at the least expense. So colleges, which are as yet only considering the two-year course with a certificate at the end, and not quite daring to take so radical a step, are luring these prospective students by advertising the number of courses that lead directly to a job. Such advertising tends to encourage the great delusion; so that more and more young people who enter college seek only those courses with "how to do it" titles.

One illustration is enough. A student sat beside my desk a year or two ago, waiting for judgment upon a paper he had written. The work was a jumble of disordered thoughts, but in it there was a very real seeking after some philosophy of living. There were flashing bits of youthful vision here and there which made me confident that such a mind, if it were fed and disciplined, might produce fine results. We chatted about courses, until I happened to say, "It's a pity you know nothing of the old philosophers. They would help you arrange your own thoughts in more orderly fashion."

He interrupted me quickly. "Philosophy—that's a course I've heard a lot about. I wish I could take it. But Dad won't hear of it. He says, 'What'll it get you?'"

That is the slogan—"What'll it get you?" So the embryo engineer (or his parent) resents time spent on history or English literature, the future accountant wants only accountancy, the young journalist wants to be forever at his practical writing, spending as little time as possible training the mind behind the pencil; and the future young teacher—above all, the young teacher—wants to know *how* to teach. In the face of this pressure the university yields inch by inch, and course by course, until one program after another becomes little more than a trade school, and the college of liberalizing studies turns into a training place for teachers. All this would be fair enough if the college course were shortened. Four years may be too short a time in which to learn *why;* but even a single year is too long a time for learning *how.*

It is like beating with fists against a brick wall to argue with some of these depression-scared youngsters ambitious to become engineers that they need history

and economics and modern languages; or to persuade
an embryo journalist that he needs almost anything
else ahead of "writing." For if the impulse to write is
in him, and a sort of predilection for it, then a good
city editor will teach him in three weeks the tricks of
the trade; but that same editor will not have the time
to teach him the vocabularies of physics, or psychology,
or art criticism, or economics, and he needs all of them
and more in his business.

A short time ago nationally assembled newspaper
editors listened to the report of their committee on education which declared that journalism schools are
spending too much time trying to teach journalism. A
distinguished practicing engineer recently informed
the deans of engineering schools that they are teaching
too much engineering. Not many years have passed
since I heard Admiral Sims make a sharp attack upon
the curriculum of the Naval Academy, which he said
was spending three years teaching its students many
things which could be learned in three weeks on a gun
turret; and too little time teaching those things most
essential for their minds' development which they
might never again have a chance to study. It is also
worth noting here that the best private preparatory
schools, being free to choose teachers with any sort of

training, avoid those who have spent time learning how to teach.

But it is hard to convince a youngster that what he most needs are a disciplined mind and a knowledge of the theories that lie behind the skills he will later acquire. It is useless to point out that a parrot can easily learn to pronounce words, and a monkey to dip a pen into ink; but neither can learn why, so they continue to live among the lower animals.

It is hard enough to convince the youngsters of this, but it is harder still, or impossible to convince their parents. "My girl has got to earn her living by teaching after I have bought an education for her; tell her how!" "My boy has got to sell real estate or write advertising after he gets out; tell him how!" And depression-scared colleges and universities all over the country are answering by printed catalogue and circular letter and recruiting lecturer: "All right. Send them along. We'll tell 'em how."

"This course teaches," says a university catalogue, "not only how to write a successful short story, but how to market it." So the world will fill up with folks who can tell stories beautifully, but have nothing to tell; and high-power salesmen who can sell anything but can't explain the trouble with it; and lawyers who know the tricks of the trade but not the ideals of the profession; and preachers with beautiful enunciation; and teachers who can't get along without textbooks. It is not the business of an undergraduate college to teach the tricks of any trade. Its business is to train brains.

Many years ago in one of the old New England colleges there were four students in residence who went out into the teaching profession and distinguished themselves as historians. Their preëminence was recognized the world over. Four decades later the newly elected president of that little college had the notion that he might induce history to repeat itself. "I shall study the old catalogues," he said to himself, "and inquire about the teaching method of that bygone day and see whether I cannot reproduce the classroom environment that sent those young men out into the history-teaching field with such enthusiasm and so brilliantly equipped." So he got out the old catalogues, and found that when those men were undergraduate students, history was not taught there at all. *Quod erat demonstrandum. Nux vomica. E pluribus unum.*

The broad background of "culture" and the discipline of mind provided by the small colleges of yesterday and a few of today are being set on a back shelf; and in the university showcases are now displayed a lot of shiny new "special trainings" for this job and that; recipes which may be memorized. The great delusion is no longer a delusion. To lure customers we will provide with each purchase a little culturine, which looks a good deal like culture if it is not tested too severely.

XXIX

So This Is Hell!

THE notebook is soiled and torn, but still legible. They say I was clinging to it even after the wheels of the truck went over me. Only the first page is undecipherable, though the last line or two seem to suggest a journey's end. From that point I shall transcribe it all, without additions or corrections.

And then the great room. [So the second page begins.] I cannot indicate its size because my own dazed impression of it seemed to vary with every wandering glance. It had an air of conservatism; one sensed that behind it stood "big business," rather than anything cheap or shoddy. Richly furnished, with many windows, many filing cabinets, many clerks who seemed never to glance my way as they went quietly about their business; and one large central desk simply furnished with the usual things. No littered papers, but several pneumatic tubes that clicked softly as they discharged or received their burdens.

At this desk sat a personage who, after my swift glimpse of his surroundings, focused all my attention. A successful business man, one would say, of admirable type, perfectly tailored for office hours, graying hair, firm jaw, forehead deeply lined. There was about him a suggestion of efficiency and power; though his only task seemed to be the swift appraisal of cards which were discharged into his desk-basket in an intermittent stream, the penciling of endorsements on each, and the return of it to another tube, or the placing of it in the hands of a summoned attendant who hurried away on silent feet.

As no one came to ask my business, I hesitantly approached this desk. The man looked up, and it was then I decided he was not old. Eyes like the black ice over a mountain stream, cold, opaque,—with a hint of prisoned forces beneath.

"Well?"

"I am looking for the devil"—somewhat tremulously I unlimbered a pencil and notebook, reporter fashion, and my hand shook as our eyes met so directly.

"Well?"

"I am here for information"—my purpose at the moment seemed only hazily defined—"I think I have been sent in advance of some one who wishes to know if he is to follow—"

"Yes, I know. I was expecting you."

"Where am I?"

"You may look about you," and he motioned toward the nearest window.

I stepped over to the heavy hangings and parted them. I was evidently on a ground floor, and looked out upon city streets, shops, buildings, normal sidewalk throngs and street traffic.

"I don't recognize it exactly," I said, turning toward him, "but it might be anywhere."

"Anywhere," he said, continuing steadily at his work.

I crossed the room to the first of many windows on the other side. Oddly enough, here was a village street with the normal complement of folk,—farmers driving to market, corner loafers, neighbors lingering at a gate.

"But it might be any place—"

"Any place," he echoed in the same even tone.

My reporter's training had overcome diffidence, and I was at his desk again. "This is Hell?" I asked.

"If you think so," and there was the motion of a smile about his lips, although his eyes did not change.

"But hell fire, and all that? I always supposed—"

He interrupted. "If you will pardon me while I attend to a momentary pressure of work; there has been an epidemic in Siam, and the cards come in more rapidly. But I shall be glad to give you full attention in a few moments."

I turned again to the first window. "Something's going on," I thought; for there was just such a throng as Broadway holds in a rush hour. I looked between high buildings into a street whose crowding procession seemed, strangely enough, to come directly at me; yet the building I was in apparently did not block traffic. It must have been of shadowy substance, standing in the heart of a great city, whose people neither saw it nor were inconvenienced by it. Motor cars, buses, jostling pedestrians moved toward me or away from me as though their paths led directly through the space I occupied.

An idea came to me with sudden shock, and I strained forward. There were two sorts of people in that crowd; some moved along in the normal way of a sidewalk throng, merely jostling one another. But a far greater number moved directly forward without avoiding those who approached, and—there is no other way to describe it—collided and passed on through. They were shadows, and yet they seemed as clearly defined and as normal as all the others. Looking more closely I thought I could see about them a sort of shimmery encircling atmosphere, like the effects of heat above a radiator.

Again I glanced back into the room. He was still at work,—calmly, quietly, no waste motion. The peace and stillness of the room was oppressive; and yet there was certainly an undercurrent of sound,—a steady mutter, a sort of far-off whisper, like many waters. But evidently my questions must wait, and I parted the curtains again.

Close to the window, against the curb, a large truck had stopped, drawn by horses. At the bridle of one stood a man who had had some trouble with his team. He had driven a heavy fist against the jaw of the plunging animal, and then I saw his boot swing against its belly. Then some impulse led him to glance for an instant directly toward me, and the look in his eyes stirred me even more than his brutality. It suggested utter despair. Then he turned, drove home another blow, made his way to the wheel and climbed to the driver's seat. In doing so he crowded against another driver who sat in a half doze, seemingly unaware of this shadowy companion.

In the sidewalk stream I noted a portly figure in the dress of a churchman,—"a bishop at least," I thought. There was ruddy skin suggesting worldly comfort, a pursey mouth easily adjusted to benediction or reproof, the characterless face of an old actor, who has played so many characters that evidence of his own no longer shows. I saw that he, too, was shadowy, and my eyes followed him, until three other figures caught my attention. They were just such a group as one meets now and then in any city, advertising themselves by dress and manner as "artistic." The man wore a wide-brimmed hat, untidy locks reaching to his coat-collar, and soft shirt open at the throat. With him were two young women, and all three were boisterously pushing through the crowd. As they drew close, and as though at a signal, the gaze of all three was full upon me, and in the eyes of the man and one of the women there was that same look of helpless terror. But the face of the third was that of a laughing girl, who seemed all un-aware of her companions.

The manager had left his desk and was standing beside me, looking out upon the scene. "Do you know now what you want to ask?" he said, "for I can give you only a moment or two."

"All those people outside—both kinds—seem to be going along freely, as though they were doing just what they have always done. I always thought people who came here went into cells, or—"

"Furnaces," he supplied, with that same empty motion of a smile. "Little devils armed with hot pitchforks shoving them in. Yes, I know; but you would find that more merciful."

"It's plain enough they suffer," I said; "I have seen their eyes. But how?"

"They do what they have always done, and can never stop, though now they have wisdom."

We watched for a moment in silence. The sight of a policeman strolling along prompted another question. "I see no police, no guards, among the shades. All seem to be doing whatever they do without compulsion?"

"It is seldom necessary," he answered shortly; "the chains of old earthly habits are even harder for a shadow-will to break."

"Can they be broken?"

"It has been known to happen."

"There is so much I want to ask. There was a man abusing a horse—"

"Yes. He must keep on, although he no longer desires to; although he most terribly desires to stop." The tone of voice had deepened and it sounded infinitely weary.

"I thought I saw a bishop," I said. "He certainly looked like a bishop, and he seemed contented enough, strolling along and nodding to people in a benevolent sort of way. But I saw his eyes. How can what he is doing now be any sort of punishment?"

"How! He must wear his air of benevolence, and his manner of self-satisfaction, and keep on uttering his precise little admonitions. Year after year, age after age, he must sonorously affirm his belief in trivialities; all the time knowing the waste and cruelty of it, putting stones into mouths opened for bread."

While he was speaking I noticed again that undercurrent of steady sound. "Do I hear machinery here somewhere, or rushing water?"

"Talkers," he said sharply. "The world's empty talkers. Men who said in a thousand words what might be said in ten. Legislators who dammed the currents of progress with words and more words. They are segregated here, drowning out one another, running on futilely, though they passionately desire time to think and to do."

"After all," I said, with more cheerfulness than I had yet felt in that place, "it isn't so terrible, if being forced to keep on in their old ways is all that men will suffer here for any kind of sin."

"Sin!" he mimicked my tone. "How men mouth that word! There is but one 'kind of sin'—to take without giving. In their life-time they never gave, and now the power of giving is gone from them."

My spirits had risen considerably. There was something illogical about it all, if only I could rid myself of the sight of all those weary, frightened eyes, and think straight. "But there are artists here, or poets,—that sort of person. Surely a poet only gives. There is a picture-house," I added, "and shadow people going in. What men put on canvas or the printed page or the screen you must admit is given to the world, and not taken from it."

He smiled coldly. "Those men who go into that picture-house day after day made the stuff they must see there. Your world has many poets, painters, novelists, biographers, dramatists, teachers, who give it nothing, but only take and take."

"Teachers?" I questioned.

"They crowd us to capacity—reciting old lectures, mouthing old maxims, following dead rituals."

The manager turned as he spoke, and I followed him. As he seated himself once more, the elusive question took form in my mind.

"The innocent," I said, "they have to be here too, or how can the sinner continue to act against them?"

"They are the living," he answered. "As they work out their destinies, they are unaware that the fists of shadows strike their cheeks, or that angry wraiths block their paths."

"Totally unaware?" I asked, for it seemed to me that I had seen again and again in that mingled throng a look of wonder on the face of some solid being as he turned in half response toward the shadow beside him.

"Not totally unaware. You yourself may have known those moments when the will was weak, and you felt yourself beset, you knew not whence or how."

I could see from the way he glanced at his work that I had reached the limit of my time. But there was one more question, though I shrank from it. "And you," I said; "you and those who help you—are not what I had expected. This is a pleasant place to work in," and I glanced around. Then I met his eyes once more, and I can never forget the look of misery and terror in them.

"Pleasant?" and the finger-tips resting on the desk were white from pressure. "Day after day after day, for what you call eternity I do what I did when I had the freedom of choice, in my years of training and testing. I too gave nothing, but took and took and took to feed my pride."

"What did you do?" I faltered.

"In a high place I dealt out what I called justice, untempered by mercy."

I had no desire to prolong the interview. In fact if I could but lose the memory of that look I should be content. "You have been very kind," I said; then with a feeble attempt at humor, "and you have shown mercy at least to one poor inquirer."

"In your case," he said coldly, "I have not yet complete jurisdiction. You will be shown the way out," he added with grave courtesy, and turned again to his cards.

I experienced an odd confusion of mind, then. Vaguely I saw that some attendants had approached. A voice said quietly, "Where in hell is my fountain pen?" There was a familiar ring to it. I must have closed my eyes for a moment, and I heard that same voice continuing, "Well, we've done a pretty good job on him, nurse. Pulled him through from the other side. He had gone completely over, or I'm no guesser."

I opened my eyes, and there beside me was our family doctor. But I still held my notebook.

XXX

Requiescat sub Silva

I⊤ was an averagely prosperous New England town but even my prejudiced Yankee eyes could not find it averagely attractive. That part which age might have beautified was unkempt. The newer part was garish and unlovely. But one feature of it all lent beauty to the neighborhood and brought joy to the beholder. Close behind the town was a hillside with a grove of oak and maple marching in fine dignity and autumn mantled beauty up its slope. The trees seemed of varying age. Those at the center towered high; about them circled many of lesser growth, shading off into saplings, and they in turn were bordered by the softer tints of seed-lings.

The spot was not hard to reach. The street I was on led almost directly toward it. I passed through a tattered fringe of business section; the street became a roadway, began an upward slope and ended at a well-kept low fence and gate. Here I found an aged retainer raking a path.

"Who owns the estate up there?" I asked.

"Town owns it," he replied, still raking.

"Is there a poor house or hospital or something, over the hill?"

"They ain't any buildin'," he answered; "it's our cemetery."

"But I don't see any monuments."

"They ain't any stuns or monyments." The man was grinning. He evidently enjoyed my surprise. "Want to take a look through, an' I'll tell ye about it. I'm hired by the caretaker." He led me through leaf-carpeted aisles to the foot of a stalwart oak. Between extended roots I saw a bronze tablet. "Read 'er," said my guide.

"Planted to the memory of Ephraim Pease who was born Nov. 9, 1796, and regretfully departed this world March 1, 1877, wishing to leave it even better than he found it."

"Tell me," I demanded.

The ancient settled himself upon a cushion of grass and proceeded to thumb tobacco into a cob pipe. "Ephrum was a queer old feller," he began. "Made a fortune in graveyard monyments, an' got's so's he hated 'em. I remember way back when I was a little cuss an' he was still doin' some of his own cuttin', I used to see him laffin' at the things folks wanted cut on the stuns. He used to say it was usually the biggest fool wanted the highest monyment. Dunno why folks 'ud patronize him, but they did from all around the township. He gave good value fer their money, I must say. But he got queerer as he got older. Used ter say funerals an' graveyards was heathenish. The minister preached agin him an' his notions when Ephrum was about seventy, an' he asked fer a copy of the sermon. Said it would be a valyble document in a few years!"

The old caretaker paused to relight his pipe. "Ephrum died when he was eighty-one, an' he left a will. Some will! He'd bought this hill pasture, an' he left it to the township fer a cemetery, free an' clear, with an annual income fer its upkeep, an' a good salary fer a caretaker who had to know about trees. But here was the trick in the thing. Anybody buried here couldn't have no stun er monyment, an' no real humped-up grave. Jest level the ground an' plant a tree, an' then he could have an inscription on a tablet not more than one foot square at the foot of it. If the tree died the deceased's folks could plant another, but the care-taker,—*forester*, the will called him,—could say what kind not to plant.

"Everybody said they wa'n't nobody goin' to be buried here; but that's where the joke come in. Folks in these parts is jest a might close. Plots here didn't cost naw-thin', so pretty soon when anybody in this town died, unless thar was suthin' in the will agin it, his folks decided to put him here. Then after a few years, the place got to be so admired by visitors that the town got kinda proud of it. Sorta bragged about it as if 'twas the town's own notion. Old Ephrum's younger brother showed up from the West later on—he was remembered in the will—an' he stuck up fer it from the first. When he died he provided fer an' apple tree an' said the town kids should be allowed to hook the apples. It's over there on the west edge; it's ben replaced once er twice, an' thar's quite an orchard round it.

"Funny thing, too"—the old man's voice was dwindling off into faintness,—"this side the hill ain't washed away at all like the other side, an' thar's a good spring with clean water thet don't never dry up."

The story ended in silence. I shook myself, and looked around. On every side of me were grave-stones in ordered rows, varied occasionally by ornate tombs and unlovely monuments. Stiff paths wound among them, and in spite of evident care there was a littered untidy look, due to broken vases on recent graves, faded and neglected flags on little sticks, and decayed wreaths or bunches of rusty everlasting. Near me sat an old man, with a cob pipe in his mouth and an aggrieved look on his face. "Guess ye went to sleep," he said. "I was jest tellin' ye some of the important stuns, whar the inscriptions is wore out. Of course only a few of the really old ones stays. If a family don't keep a grave up, it gits leveled off in time. Even the fancy ones, folks can't always remember now why they was so fancy. Wal, even the best of us gits fergotten," he added with a sort of mournful satisfaction.

I turned and glanced at the ornate monument against which I was resting. The old man noted my action. "Funny about that one," he said. "Old feller made a lot of money out of grave-stuns. I was tellin' ye about him when ye was asleep"—there was again a hint of grievance in his tone; "I guess all the mony-ments around here with urns an' weeping willers on 'em was made by him. His plot looks tidier than most the other old ones; he provided fer that in his will. But I guess thar ain't nobody in town remembers him. His folks is all dead an' gone."

I looked with curiosity at the inscription: "sacred to the memory of Ephraim Pease, who was born Nov. 9, 1796, and departed this life Mar. 1, 1877, in the hope of a blessed resurrection. He gladly left this vale of sin a better world to enter in."

THE END